THE

MISSION OF JESUS

DISCOVERY GUIDE

That the World May Know® with Ray Vander Laan

THE
MISSION
OF JESUS

—— 5 LESSONS ON ——

**Triumph of God's Kingdom
in a World of Chaos**

DISCOVERY GUIDE

**EXPERIENCE THE BIBLE IN
HISTORICAL CONTEXT™**
Ray Vander Laan
With Stephen and Amanda Sorenson

ZONDERVAN

The Mission of Jesus Discovery Guide
Copyright © 2016 by Ray Vander Laan

This title is also available as a Zondervan ebook. Visit www.zondervan.com/ebooks.

Requests for information should be addressed to:
Zondervan, 3900 *Sparks Dr. SE, Grand Rapids, Michigan 49546*

Focus on the Family and the accompanying logo and design are federally registered trademarks of Focus on the Family, 8605 Explorer Drive, Colorado Springs, Colorado 80920.

That the World May Know and Faith Lessons are trademarks of Focus on the Family.

ISBN 978-0-310-81221-0

All maps created by International Mapping.

All photos, unless otherwise indicated, are courtesy of Ray Vander Laan, Paul Murphy, and Grooters Productions.

Cover design: Zondervan
Cover photography: Grooters Productions
Interior design: Denise Froehlich

First Printing May 2016 / Printed in the United States of America

CONTENTS

INTRODUCTION

More than two thousand years ago, a young Jewish woman named Mary with no place to call home found shelter in a shepherd's cave, or in a stable beneath a home, and gave birth to a son. With the birth of that child, God took the most significant step in his great plan to redeem a broken world. It was not the first step in his plan to reclaim his world, nor would it be the last.

From the beginning, God had entrusted to his human partners a mission to fill the earth, use it wisely, and rule it well.[1] This mission was disrupted when Adam and Eve sinned, but God did not give up on choosing people to be his partners in blessing and reclaiming his creation.[2] Long before Mary made her way to Bethlehem, God's people had been part of a journey of redemption that had spanned more than a millennium. People such as Abraham and Sarah, Moses, Rahab, Ruth, David and Bathsheba, Elijah, and Isaiah had shared in the responsibility of being God's partners — his instruments in bringing the good news of redemption to the world around them.

God chose and entrusted the Promised Land to the Jewish people not only to provide for their daily bread but to give them a platform from which to fulfill their mission of displaying him to a watching world. The *Via Maris,* one of the great ancient trade routes, stretched from Egypt to Babylon and passed through the Promised Land. God placed the Israelites on the crossroads of the world, intending for them to take control of the cities along this route, serve him faithfully, and thereby influence the surrounding nations.

To some extent, Israel made God known to people from many nations as they traveled the *Via Maris.* In profound ways Israel also would experience and influence the great empires at both ends of the *Via Maris.* When God redeemed Israel from slavery in Egypt, the Egyptians and their king, Pharaoh, learned the nature of the Creator of the universe and his desire to redeem his creation.[3]

The Assyrian dispersion and the Babylonian exile had also spread God-fearing Jewish people around the known world.

Yet the chaos of sin still reigned in the world. Had God's plan failed because his people often failed? Was the baby Mary placed in the manger a replacement program for the failed efforts of his people?

The answer is *no*. Although God's people often failed to carry out the mission he had for them, they were not failures. God used them to prepare carefully and well for the next step in his great plan of restoration: a redemptive mission that his Son alone — no human partners — could accomplish. All that had come before was preparation for the birth of that baby in the shepherd's cave whose atoning death and resurrection are the only source of restored relationship with God our Creator.

The Mission of Israel Continued in Jesus

It is important to remember there was more to Jesus' life on earth than the salvation accomplished through his suffering, death, and resurrection. Yes, Jesus is Savior and no one comes to the Father except through him. His redemptive mission dealt with the guilt of human sin, defeated the power of the Evil One, and healed and reconciled all creation to the Creator. We will investigate how Jesus came to fully accomplish God's plan of redemption as Savior and Lord by his death, resurrection, and ascension.

God also entrusted to his Son the very mission he had given to Israel: to be the light that would make God known to all nations. So we will join Jesus in his ministry to see how he embodied that mission. We will come to know Jesus as the light of the world[4] who came to reveal the Father[5] and make God's name known. We will see how Jesus, by his words and actions, displayed the nature of God as Creator, owner and ruler of all. We will see how knowing Jesus makes it possible to know the Father.[6]

We will follow Jesus in Galilee as he sailed across the sea and restored a man possessed by a legion of demons. Out of compassion for a deeply troubled man, Jesus challenged the power of the Evil One and made God known to the Gentile inhabitants of a Roman province. We will join the Gospel account of Jesus' crucifixion by the authority of Imperial Rome. We will visit Rome itself, wondering how believers there explained his death to their Roman neighbors. We will stand on the Mount of Olives and consider the story of Jesus' ascension to be enthroned at God's right hand and given all authority in heaven and on earth — a story much like the one circulating in the Roman world concerning Julius Caesar's ascension. In each of these studies we will consider both aspects of Jesus' mission: his suffering and death for our salvation and his embodiment of Israel's mission to be a light to the nations.

The Text in Its Context

Our study will focus on the Bible (also referred to as Scripture or the Text), the record of God reclaiming and restoring his broken world. Having studied in the Jewish world, I believe it is important to communicate clearly how the nature of that inspired book is understood. Although it is in some ways helpful to speak in terms of "Old" and "New" Testaments, such descriptions can also be misleading if they are interpreted to mean old and outdated and the new replacement. Nothing, in my opinion, is further from the truth. The "New" Testament describes the great advance of God's plan with the arrival of the Messiah and the promise of his continued and completed work.[7] The "Old" presents the foundational events and people God used to advance his work. The Bible is not complete without both Testaments. It is one Bible, one plan to reclaim God's world, one way to be restored to harmony with him, one people, one revelation. To focus on that unity, I prefer to refer to the Hebrew Text (Old Testament) and the Christian Text (New Testament), which together are the inspired, infallible Word of God.

The message of the Scriptures is, of course, eternal and unchanging, but the circumstances and conditions of the people of the Bible are unique to their times, and their contributions clearly bear the stamp of time and place. Most inspired human writers of the Bible, as well as those to whom the words were originally given, were Jews living in the ancient Near East. God's words and actions spoke to them with such power, clarity, and purpose that they carefully preserved them as an authoritative body of literature. In order to deepen our understanding of God's Word and fully apply the message of the Bible to our lives, we must enter the world of the Bible and familiarize ourselves with its culture. By learning how to think and approach life as Abraham, Moses, Ruth, John the Baptist, and Paul did, modern Christians deepen their appreciation of God's Word.

From the beginning, God spoke and acted within the context of the human cultures in which his people lived. Without advocating any pagan practices or beliefs, God frequently communicated his message through culturally familiar metaphors that made the meaning and point of his message strikingly clear and relevant. Abraham cut up animals to create a blood covenant much as the ruling Hittites did. The design of the temple of the Lord in Jerusalem, built by Solomon, had a design similar to that of temples used by neighboring cultures. In Corinth, where clay and marble replicas of various body parts were sculpted and displayed as votive offerings to the pagan god of healing, Paul described the community of faith as a body made up of many parts.

Understanding the Scriptures involves more than knowing what words mean; it involves understanding those words and images within the context in which God spoke and acted and from the life perspective of the people with whom he communicated. Biblical writers assumed that their readers were familiar with Near Eastern language, geography, history, and culture. Unfortunately, many Christians do not have even a basic knowledge of the world and people of the Bible. So we will be studying the people and events of the Bible in their geographical, historical, and cultural contexts. Once we know the who, what, when, and where of a Bible story, we will be able to understand the why and gain a clearer understanding of God's revelation.

As we consider God's practice of communicating through a cultural setting, we must be careful to avoid two extremes of interpretation when we study God's Word. First, we must recognize that our own culture shapes how we interpret the text and that the ancient culture likely differs significantly from our own. Second, we must guard against "canonizing" the ancient culture by insisting that God's people today practice their faith in the same way as ancient people did. Both extremes miss the point that the cultural setting in which God placed his revelation is a useful tool for understanding the message and application of the text.[8]

The people God chose to be his instruments — the people to whom he revealed himself — typically described their world in concrete terms. Their language was one of pictures, metaphors, and examples rather than ideas, definitions, and abstractions. Whereas we might describe God as omniscient or omnipresent (knowing everything and present everywhere), they would have preferred to describe God by saying, "The Lord is my Shepherd." Thus, the Bible is filled with concrete images: God is our Father, and we are his children. God is the Potter, and we are the clay. Jesus is the Lamb killed on Passover. The kingdom of heaven is like the yeast a woman took and mixed into flour. Furthermore, faith as action receives a greater emphasis than does faith as rational concept. The way to know God is to observe him in action rather than attempting to define him by doctrine.

For this reason, the ancient stories are more than simply history. God's great redemptive acts were remembered and constantly retold because he is known by what he does. The stories of God and his people in action define our faith — the God we serve and the walk he desires. We don't simply know the story, we join the story.

Understanding the walk God desires is not simply memorizing laws, rules, and regulations but remembering how we — always *we* — lived in the past both obediently and disobediently. We were slaves in Egypt, we heard God at Sinai, we journeyed through the desert, we worshiped idols, and we repented and were restored. Paul describes this Jewish approach to godly living by writing, "these things occurred as examples."[9]

In addition, Eastern thought emphasizes the process of learning as much or more than the end result. Whereas Westerners tend to collect information to find the right answer, Hebrew thought stresses the process of discovery as well as the answer — or better — learning how to find right answers.

We must remember that Jesus, too, spoke and acted within the context of the culture of his day. He was a first-century Jew from Nazareth whose words, actions, and teaching methods were in keeping with the customs, traditions, and religious practices of the Jewish culture into which he was born. He lived like a Jew, talked like a Jew, acted like a Jew, and worshiped like a Jew. He was born into a land that was in political and religious turmoil, where the rocky soil was stained red with the blood of the conquered and the conquerors, a land that for centuries had been the crossroads of the world.

Like many people of his time, Jesus knew the harshness of Roman overlords and the corruption of religious leadership. He knew hard work as a stonemason or builder. He knew what it meant to lead sheep, catch fish, and experience everyday life in a Galilean household. His sandaled feet got dusty and dirty; he perspired and got thirsty in the burning sun of the Judean wilderness. None of this diminishes our Messiah. It makes the fact that he was willing to experience it for us, in a difficult time and place, all the more amazing.

The Land in Perspective

Western Christianity tends to spiritualize the application of the Promised Land as it is presented in the Bible. Instead of hearing God's call to live publicly and passionately in order to influence the culture around them, modern Christians often view the Promised Land as a distant heavenly city, a glorious "Canaan" toward which we are traveling as we ignore the world around us. We tend to focus on the destination, not the journey, and in so doing have unconsciously separated our walk with God from our responsibility toward the world in which he has placed us. Our earthly experience is reduced to preparation for an eternity in the "promised land."

Preoccupation with this idea distorts the mission God has given us. Our mission is the same one God gave to the Israelites. We are to live obediently within the world so that through us all nations may know that our God is the one true God. Living by faith is not a vague, otherworldly experience. Rather, it is being faithful to God right now, in the place and time he has put us. God wants his people in the game, not on the bench. I pray that seeing the Bible in the context in which God placed its stories and characters will help you to understand how to respond to his revelation with a greater passion for faithfulness.

This study was filmed in several locations in Israel and Rome. However, these are modern political designations and we will refer to their biblical names in the study itself. Several terms are used to identify the land God promised to Abraham. The Hebrew Text refers to it as Canaan or Israel. The Christian Text calls it Judea. After the Second Jewish Revolt (AD 132 – 135), it was known as Palestine. Each of these names resulted from historical events taking place in the land at the time the terms were coined.

Canaan is one of the earliest designations of the Promised Land. It probably meant "purple," referring to the dye produced from the shells of murex shellfish along the coast of Phoenicia. In the ancient world, this famous dye was used to color garments worn by royalty, and the word for the color referred to the people who produced the dye and purple cloth for trade. Hence, *Canaanite* refers to a "trader" or "merchant" as well as to a person from the "land of purple," or Canaan.

Israel, the Hebrew Text designation for the Promised Land, derives from the patriarch Jacob, whom God renamed Israel (Genesis 32:28). His descendants were known as the children of Israel. After the Israelites conquered Canaan during the time of Joshua, the name of the people became the designation for the land (as it had with the Canaanites). When the nation split following the death of Solomon, the northern kingdom and its territory was called Israel while the southern land was called Judah. After the fall of the northern kingdom to the Assyrians in 722 BC, the entire land was again called Israel.

Palestine comes from the people of the coastal plain, the Philistines. Although the Egyptians used *Palestine* long before the Roman period to refer to the land where the Philistines lived, Roman Emperor Hadrian popularized the term as part of his campaign to eliminate Jewish influence in the area (about one hundred years after Jesus' death). At the time of Jesus, the Promised Land was called *Judea* (meaning "Jewish"), which technically referred to the land that had been the nation of Judah. Because of the influence the people of Judea exerted over the rest of the land, it was called Judea. The Romans divided the land into a number of provinces: Judea, Samaria, and Galilee (the three main divisions during Jesus' time); Gaulanitis, the Decapolis, and Perea (east of the Jordan River); and Idumaea (Edom) and Nabatea (in the south). These further divisions add to the rich historical and cultural background God prepared for the coming of Jesus and the beginning of his church.

Today the names *Israel* and *Palestine* are often used to designate the land God gave to Abraham. Both terms are politically charged. *Palestine* is used by the Arabs living in the central part of the country, while *Israel* is used by the Jews to indicate the modern political State of Israel. In this study, *Israel* is used not to indicate a political statement regarding the current struggle in the Middle East but to best reflect the biblical designation for the land.

The Mission for All God's People

After Jesus' ascension, his mission — Israel's mission — continued for all of his followers. The people of God were to live so that the world would know God — not just in one small place but throughout the entire world.

> *Then Jesus came to them and said, "All authority in heaven and on earth has been given to me. Therefore go and make disciples of all nations, baptizing them in the name of the Father and of the Son and of the Holy Spirit, and teaching them to obey everything I have commanded you. And surely I am with you always, to the very end of the age."*
>
> *Matthew 28:18 – 20*

Jesus' followers in the early church would reveal him to people in such cities as Rome and Athens and in such Roman provinces as Syria and Macedonia. The most pagan of all provinces, Asia Minor, would become a stronghold for the followers of God and Jesus. They would serve him while the nations of the world watched and listened.

Now it is our turn. We who have been redeemed by the blood of Jesus are called and empowered to make known to the nations the good news of his redemptive power. Like Israel, we must join the mission to become God's light to the nations — his priests who hallow his name so that his kingdom will come as his will is done. We are to declare the good news of his saving work. We are to live as concrete examples of knowing God and displaying him by our words and actions. At every point in our study, we will be challenged to take our place as God's partners in that mission.

I often hear people give a somber critique of Western culture, noting its seemingly inevitable decline toward secularism and paganism. This approach is unfortunate, to say the least, because God's desire for all creation to come to know him — experience him — has not diminished. Never has there been a greater opportunity to be God's coworkers,[10] to mediate his presence, to be a kingdom of priests who make him known to a world in spiritual darkness.

Through the mission of Abraham and Sarah, God promised that all nations would be blessed.[11] Israel, although sometimes rebellious and unwilling to be God's faithful partner, became a blessing to others. Non-Hebrews joined them when they left Egypt. Tamar, Rahab, and Ruth came to know the God of Israel and joined his community. The entire city of Nineveh was spared God's judgment because he sent Jonah to warn them and they repented. God's blessing to Abraham became their mission as well.

Then Jesus, who Matthew traces back to Abraham,[12] was born. In Jesus, God's promise to bless all nations through Abraham is revealed in all its fullness. Matthew ends Jesus' story with the Great Commission in which the good news is to be dispersed to all nations. Thus Jesus is both the one who carries out the mission to make God known and the one whose redemptive work is the blessing promised to all nations.

God's partners have always struggled to carry out their task faithfully. For many who follow Jesus today, the temptation is to become so much like the culture we seek to influence that we have little effect on it. Others of us seek isolation from a broken world in places that we deem "safe to raise children" and thereby miss opportunities to make God known to those who are alienated from him.

I hope and pray that many of us will engage our culture as a minority,[13] seeking the welfare of the culture in which God has placed us. We do not have to be powerful or a majority to accomplish the mission God has given to us! Christianity, like Judaism, has had its finest hours when it was a poor and weak minority committed to carrying out God's mission to a broken world. The early church, a powerless minority in the world of Imperial Rome, exerted a dramatic impact by being faithful to God and his calling. So we must be as well.[14]

CAPERNAUM: JESUS BINDS THE EVIL ONE

Years after Jesus ascended to heaven, Paul explained to Jesus-followers in the province of Galatia that God had chosen Israel, the descendants of Abraham, to be the instrument of God's blessing to all nations.[1] Although God's chosen people were not always faithful to their calling, many Jews eagerly tried to be the people God had called them to be. As history progressed, they played a significant role in preparing for the coming Messiah. They slowly matured until "when the set time had fully come, God sent his Son"![2] The Messiah would be born on earth to fulfill his role in bringing God's promised blessing to all nations.

In part because of the oppressive Roman regime that governed them, the Jews of Jesus' day longed for the arrival of the promised Messiah. They hoped for a Savior who would restore their freedom and enable them once again to be God's light to the nations. Many Jews responded positively to John the Baptizer's message calling them to repent — turn back to God's path — because the Messiah's coming was imminent.[3] Many also had an intense desire to understand and obey God's revealed Scriptures and diligently studied the Text. Itinerant teachers called "rabbis" or "honored teachers" traveled from village to village explaining and applying the scroll of the Torah, the Prophets, and the Writings.

It is likely that God's people had never been more literate in the Scriptures, more passionate about obeying God, or better prepared to receive Jesus' message than the day Mary laid her baby in the manger in Bethlehem.

Although some Judeans disdained what they perceived to be a provincial and backward Galilean culture,[4] the opposite is likely true. Due to their proximity to trade routes, Galileans were exposed to the Gentile world more than Judeans, who generally resided in more isolated mountain locations. Furthermore, the standard of religious education in Galilee was superior to that of the Judean community as a whole. More well-known, first-century rabbis came from Galilee than from anywhere else in the Jewish world.[5]

Even ordinary Galileans participated in organized study of the Torah and other texts. They engaged in lively discussion and debate over the smallest details and interpretation of the Text so they would know how to obey God's Word. Memorization of Scripture was a significant part of their children's education. Consequently, almost everyone was so familiar with the Text that a rabbi could allude to a passage simply by using a word or phrase from it and assume that his hearers would have that passage in mind and apply it to his teaching. This was the religious environment in which Jesus grew up.

Like many faithful Jews, Galileans passionately longed for the coming of the kingdom of heaven — the restoration of God's reign over the Promised Land and eventually the entire world. Many believed that when Messiah arrived he would orchestrate a violent overthrow of their Roman masters. They expected a complete reversal of power much like what took place when Joshua led the Israelites to take possession of the Promised Land a millennium earlier. So when Jesus proclaimed that the kingdom of God had come,[6] his hearers no doubt were overjoyed. But given the history of how God dealt with Israel's oppressors during ancient times, they also found it difficult to accept Jesus' emphasis on the kingdom of God coming about through love and forgiveness toward one's neighbor and even one's enemy. Jesus had much to teach them about his kingdom and their role in making it known.

Opening Thoughts (3 minutes)

The Very Words of God

> *But when the set time had fully come, God sent his Son ...*
>
> *Galatians 4:4*

Think About It

We all have expectations of what being "saved" or redeemed by God will be like. Often we focus on the expectations that have to do with our eternal destiny — the promise of life in heaven with God. But let's turn our thoughts toward what redemption — being restored to the family and kingdom of God — might mean for our life on earth right now.

What do we expect life on earth to be like when God has forgiven us and restored us as his beloved children?

What are some of our expectations of life in our role as partners with God in his ongoing work of redemption?

Video Notes (31 minutes)

God's plan to redeem his creation

Jesus came and lived among us

Capernaum:

A community intent on being faithful—set apart—to God

Jesus has a message: you are set apart to go "over there"

The kingdom of God versus the strong man's kingdom

Jesus has power over the strong man's kingdom

Video Discussion (7 minutes)

1. How amazing is it for a king to leave behind the glories of his realm in order to participate in the brokenness of life with his most needy subjects?

   In what ways do you think the realization that Jesus — the King of kings — willingly did this to redeem all of humanity can help followers of Jesus today: (1) to have greater compassion for desperate, broken people? (2) to better understand our purpose as God's partners in restoring to his family those who have lost their way?

2. Why do you think it was important for Jesus to conduct his teaching ministry in the area of Capernaum, where people already took seriously the book — God's Word — and where the most dedicated Jewish scholars and teachers congregated?

3. What tensions did God-fearing Jews in Capernaum experi-
    ence regarding their call to be holy and set apart while also
    being a kingdom of priests in a pagan world of immorality,
    idolatry, and bloodshed?

    How could they be set apart and at the same time engaged
    enough in their world to display God to people who desper-
    ately needed him?

    In what way(s) do followers of Jesus today face a similar
    challenge?

4. Jesus describes the battle between good and evil in terms of
    two kingdoms in conflict — the kingdom of God versus the
    kingdom of the "strong man," the Evil One, or the kingdom
    on the "other side." How aware of these two kingdoms does
    it seem the faithful Jews of Capernaum and the surrounding
    area were?

In what ways did Jesus demonstrate his power and authority over the strong man's kingdom?

What impact might these events have had on the thoughts, feelings, and actions of Jesus' disciples and others?

How easy or difficult is it for us to broaden our perspective, comprehend the unexpected, and respond appropriately when God operates in a way we don't anticipate?

FOR GREATER UNDERSTANDING
The Decapolis — aka, the "Other Side"

Just across the Sea of Galilee from Capernaum was a region of city states known as the Decapolis. Alexander the Great originally established the ten cities of the Decapolis in lands east of the Sea of Galilee when he conquered the area in 332 BC. He founded these cities and populated them with his soldiers and their families in order to promote the Hellenistic worldview of the Greeks among the local people.

In 63 BC, under the Roman commander Pompey, the Roman Empire annexed the Decapolis and continued promoting Hellenistic culture and influence. By the time of Jesus, the ten cities had become wealthy, prosperous communities that were Greek in every way—language, lifestyle, religion. Populated mostly by Gentiles, the cities featured paved streets lined with temples, theaters, baths, arenas, shops, and public buildings. The people indulged in the hedonism of Hellenism—the pursuit of power, pleasure, and leisure.

For the religious Jews of Galilee, the Decapolis was evil and unclean. The Lord had commanded his people, as his witnesses to the nations, to "touch no unclean thing" (Isaiah 52:11). So everything about the Decapolis—its people, its practices, its property—was to be avoided at all costs. Faithful Jews would avoid even speaking the word *Decapolis* lest doing so would defile them!

THE LOCATION OF ANCIENT HIPPOS, THE DECAPOLIS CITY KNOWN BY THE JEWS AS SUSITA, CAN BE SEEN ON A HILLTOP ACROSS THE SEA OF GALILEE FROM CAPERNAUM.

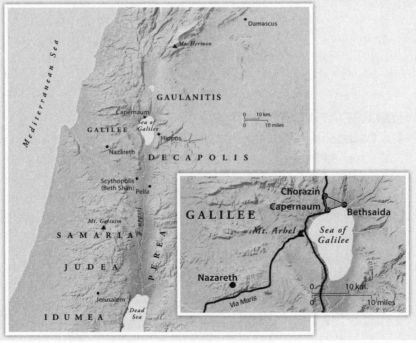

Small Group Bible Discovery and Discussion (13 minutes)

When Jesus Takes God's Kingdom to the "Other Side"

From the beginning of time when God's creative power brought order out of chaos, the Evil One has embarked on a deadly and cruel mission to destroy God's *shalom* and keep humankind in bondage to evil. This conflict was first documented in the Garden of Eden with Adam and Eve. It is evident in the spiritual conflict underlying Israel's slavery in Egypt and the ten plagues God brought against Egypt's gods. It formed the backdrop for battles between Israel and her enemies, between heroes such as David and antagonists such as Goliath. The spiritual battle between the kingdom of heaven and the kingdom of Satan is exemplified in the idolatry to which Israel was repeatedly seduced.

Since the coming of Messiah is the central event of the arrival of the kingdom reign of God, we should not be surprised that conflict between the kingdom of heaven and the kingdom of the Evil One would reach a climax. The time had fully come. The Evil One would do everything possible to prevent the kingdom of heaven — the triumphant reign of God — from defeating his evil kingdom. Consequently, as Jesus fulfilled his mission of demonstrating the kingdom of God on earth, he would confront the powers of darkness and the abyss. The Evil One and his spirits would oppose Jesus throughout his ministry in an attempt to silence the good news of the kingdom of heaven.

1. One evening, after teaching the crowds who followed him in Galilee, Jesus said to his disciples: "Let us go over to the other side" (Mark 4:35, also Luke 8:22). From what you have already discovered about Jesus' disciples and what the "other side" represented, what do you imagine they thought about Jesus' intentions? Hint: Consider what Peter said to a Roman centurion in Acts 10:28.

DATA FILE
The Sea of Galilee

The Sea of Galilee is a beautiful freshwater lake nestled in a "basin" about 700 feet below sea level, surrounded by mountains. It is nearly eight miles wide at its widest point and thirteen and a half miles long from north to south. One can see the opposite shore from anywhere on its banks. Even today it retains a calm, rural setting reminiscent of what it would have looked like during the time of Jesus. But first-century Galileans had a different view of the lake than we might realize from photographs taken on a beautiful day.

The mountains surrounding the Sea of Galilee add much to the beauty of its setting. In Galilee to the west, the hills reach nearly 1,400 feet above sea level. To the east, the mountains of the Golan Heights (the Decapolis during the time of Jesus) rise quickly to more than 2,500 feet above sea level, and beyond them is desert. Mount Arbel in Galilee and the mountains of the Golan Heights are very steep and drop sharply down to the sea.

These features contribute to volatile, severe weather on the water. When cooler air from the surrounding mountains blows over the warmer air above the Sea of Galilee, the resulting inversion — heavier, cold air dropping as warm air rises — causes sudden, violent storms. The phenomenon is particularly severe when there is an east wind. The area to the east is much higher and temperatures in the nearby desert can be very cold at night. The east wind brings this cold air over the sea where it can create waves higher than six feet in just a few minutes! The particular storm in our story must have been more intense than usual because the former fishermen thought they would die.

Although Galilean fishermen went out in boats to catch the fish the Sea of Galilee provided, the Jewish people as a culture were not entirely comfortable with the sea. Their ancestral father, Abraham, was a Negev shepherd. Their ancestors wandered in the desert for forty years before settling in the Promised Land. As a people they were desert nomads, not seafarers. They rarely controlled the seacoast, and to them the sea appeared alien and threatening. It was a symbol of chaos, a place of untamed evil and danger.

In the Bible, the imagery generally associated with the sea conveys a negative connotation. For example, Genesis 1:1 – 3 describes the world beginning as watery chaos, a primeval sea from which God brought order. The sea was a tool of God's judgment (Genesis 6–7; Exodus 14) and always remained a dangerous place (Psalm 30:1; 69:1–3). Jonah was thrown into its depths (Jonah 2:3–6) where the monster lives (Job 7:12). Based on the sea's image as the home of evil chaos that God alone can control, Daniel describes terrible beasts from the sea (Daniel 7:2–7; see also Psalm 65:5–7; 77:19; 89:9; 93:3–4; Exodus 14–15). In addition, the sea was home to the dragon, Leviathan, which symbolized pagan enemy nations (Isaiah 27:1; 51:9–10).

According to Jewish tradition, the depths of the sea are viewed as the home of demonic beings who oppose God—a place called the Abyss (a Greek term meaning "depths," which in Hebrew is "depth" or "deep"). John referred to the Abyss often in his Revelation (9:1, 11; 11:7; 17:8) as the abode of Satan (Revelation 20:1–3). Someday the devil himself will rise from the sea (Revelation 13:1–11). No wonder the disciples feared they would perish in the storm. No wonder they cried out for Jesus to save them.

2. Jesus and his disciples had a harrowing trip across the Sea of Galilee. Read Matthew 8:23 – 25 and Mark 4:35 – 38.

   a. The disciples, several of whom had been fishermen, were likely expert seamen. What indicates that this was an extraordinary experience?

   b. What was Jesus doing even during the height of the storm, and why do you think he was able to do it?

DID YOU KNOW?

Jewish writers of the Text often hint at a meaning without saying it directly. Matthew, for example, uses the word *seismos* to describe the storm on the Sea of Galilee. *Seismos* typically means an earthquake, often one that represents apocalyptic conflict between God and the forces of evil, as in Matthew 24:7; 27:51; and 28:2.

By using *seismos* to describe a storm on a lake, Matthew suggests that these events are about much more than weather and Jesus' power over it. The Evil One knew that Jesus was on a mission to challenge his kingdom. In an attempt to prevent the kingdom of heaven from advancing, the forces of hell broke loose, causing earth-shaking violence to erupt on the water. No wonder the little boat and its occupants were nearly swallowed by the sea and the power of its depths!

IMAGINE WHAT IT WOULD BE LIKE TO ENCOUNTER AN EPIC STORM IN A SMALL BOAT SUCH AS THIS!

3. When the disciples were certain they would not survive, they awakened Jesus for help. In addition to the immediate threat of the storm, what about the sea likely heightened their fear? (See Genesis 1:1 – 3; 6:11 – 13, 17; Exodus 14:26 – 28; Isaiah 27:1; Jonah 1:1 – 16.)

4. The way Jesus demonstrated his power over the storm
    revealed much more to his disciples than simply his control
    over the forces of nature. Consider what he did, how he said
    it, and what his disciples — who knew their Hebrew Bible —
    would have heard in his words. (See Mark 4:39; Luke 8:24.)

    a. What did Jesus do, and what resulted?

    b. To hear what the disciples heard in Jesus' rebuke, we
        need some background. They would have recognized
        Jesus' rebuke as an allusion to God rebuking (Hebrew:
        ga'ar) Satan in Zechariah 3:2. The Greek word *epitimao*,
        translated as "rebuke" in Mark 4:39, was used often in the
        Jewish world when commanding demons to leave people.
        Jesus, for example, would exorcise a demon (or demons)
        first by rebuking it,[7] which silenced the demon and made
        it ineffective in spreading further chaos. Then the demon
        could be driven out of the victim.[8] So when Jesus "rebuked"
        the storm, he literally commanded the storm to be silent
        and the sea to be at peace — literally "be muzzled," or in
        plain English, "shut up!"[9] When Jesus commanded the
        storm — as if it were a living being — to be silent, what was
        he revealing about the true source or power behind the
        storm? About his identity? About what might be in store for
        them when they reached the other side?

c.   In his rebuke (Mark 4:39), Jesus commanded the sea: "Quiet! Be still!" Read Psalm 65:5 – 7; 89:8 – 9; and 107:28 – 29. Who else quieted and stilled the sea with these words, and how significant is it that Jesus did the same thing?

d.   What impact did the realization of Jesus' identity and power over evil have on his disciples that night? Do you think they knew the answer to their own question? Why or why not? (See Mark 4:41.)

Faith Lesson (5 minutes)

The conflict between God's kingdom and the kingdom of the Evil One continues today. The intense storm Jesus and his disciples encountered on the Sea of Galilee represents what Satan will do to keep people in bondage and to stir up chaos that can hinder the advancement of God's kingdom. If we are determined to take the *shalom* of God's kingdom into a sinful, broken world, the Evil One will oppose us just as he opposed our Lord. He does not relinquish his kingdom or those who serve him without a fight. He may bring storms into our lives or try to persuade us to avoid even going to the "other side."

Although our adversary is not easily overcome, we must remember that God's power is far greater than that of the enemy. The Evil One may still be fighting, but he has been defeated. All of creation belongs to God, and he has entrusted his human partners to care for it. When we — who claim Jesus as our King — serve him by obeying his will in our words and actions, the kingdom of heaven grows. We bring the good news that God can bind the Evil One in any situation, deliver anyone who accepts Jesus as Savior and Lord from the Evil One's power, and bear witness to a spiritually dark world what it looks like when God's kingdom comes on earth as it is in heaven.

1. Whereas it is popular, and certainly appealing, to believe that following Jesus and proclaiming through our words, lifestyle, and actions that he is King will result in health and wealth, Scripture clearly reveals a different perspective. Those who bear witness of the kingdom of God will pass through stormy waters. Consider some of the storms — the confrontations and obstacles — that the apostle Paul encountered:

    a. When he went with what were likely Jewish believers to the temple for purification (see Acts 21:26 – 36; 22:22 – 25)

    b. When he was brought before the Sanhedrin (see Acts 22:30 – 23:2, 23:6 – 10, 12 – 15)

    c. When he departed Caesarea by ship to make his appeal to Caesar in Rome (see Acts 27:13 – 20, 33 – 44)

    d. How significant an obstacle could these circumstances have been to Paul fulfilling the mission God gave him, and why?

2. What sustained and encouraged Paul to continue sharing the message of God's kingdom to the other side during these hard times? (See Acts 18:9 – 10; 22:17 – 21; 23:11; 27:23 – 25.)

3. As you seek to walk with Jesus and obey his will, consider where the other side is for you, and what might God want you to do there that would extend his kingdom.

    a. Who are the people living in spiritual darkness around you who need to be set free from bondage to the Evil One?

    b. What specific "storms" have you faced (or are you facing) as you take back what the enemy has stolen from the kingdom of God?

Closing (1 minute)

Read Isaiah 43:10 – 12 aloud together: " 'You are my witnesses,' declares the Lord, 'and my servant whom I have chosen, so that you may know and believe me and understand that I am he. Before me no god was formed, nor will there be one after me. I, even I, am the Lord, and apart from me there is no savior. I have revealed and saved and proclaimed — I, and not some foreign god among you. You are my witnesses,' declares the Lord, 'that I am God.' "

Then pray, praising God that he is the King of kings — Creator, Redeemer, and Lord. Thank him for not giving up on us when the Evil One entices us to pursue our own way, for forgiving us, and for giving us the opportunity to be his partners in showing the world that he is God! Express your commitment to obey him in all things and thereby extend the reign of his kingdom in the spiritually dark places of this world. Ask him to give you a listening and responsive spirit so that you will be faithful in taking back territory for his kingdom.

Memorize

> *"You are my witnesses," declares the Lord, "and my servant whom I have chosen, so that you may know and believe me and understand that I am he. Before me no god was formed, nor will there be one after me. I, even I, am the Lord, and apart from me there is no savior. I have revealed and saved and proclaimed — I, and not some foreign god among you. You are my witnesses," declares the Lord, "that I am God."*
>
> **Isaiah 43:10 – 12**

The Kingdom of Heaven Advances: Reclaiming What Belongs to God

In-Depth Personal Study Sessions

Study 1 | Called to Be a Kingdom of Priests

The Very Words of God

> *Now if you obey me fully and keep my covenant, then out of all nations you will be my treasured possession. Although the whole earth is mine, you will be for me a kingdom of priests and a holy nation.*
>
> *Exodus 19:5 – 6*

Bible Discovery

"Set Apart" for a Purpose

Christians may be familiar with what is known as the "Great Commission" when Jesus sent his disciples into the world to proclaim his gospel (Matthew 28:18 – 20), but many do not realize that God gave Israel a "Great Commission" too. When God redeemed his people from bondage in Egypt and led them to Mount Sinai, he commissioned them to "obey me fully and ... be for me a kingdom of priests and a holy nation" (Exodus 19:5 – 6). By being his "priests" in their world, Israel would demonstrate the good news of God's kingdom.

It is important for followers of Jesus today to understand Israel's mission and how God intends it to be accomplished because Jesus' mission on earth and the mission he gave to his disciples are extensions of the mission God originally assigned to Israel. God wants to be known by all nations, and he wants his people to convey his message by functioning as a kingdom of priests who demonstrate accurately who he is to a watching world.[10] In order to fulfill that mission, God's people must be holy and distinct from their pagan neighbors — set apart by virtue of their faithful, obedient devotion to God and all of his commands. Only then can they fulfill the role of priests who display, or mediate, God to the world around them. Unholy priests cannot display God as he truly is. We must consider what it means to be a priest who puts God on display and by doing so extends God's reign on earth.

DID YOU KNOW?

At Mount Sinai, God used the familiar role of priests to help Israel understand their role in fulfilling his great plan of redemption. God commissioned the Israelites to be priests to the world as Israel's priests were to Israel. They were to represent him and his kingdom not only by sharing his message through what they said but by *being* his message — displaying God by the way they lived. Their role as God's holy priests was to:

- *Mediate* between God and people
- *Demonstrate* what God is like in word and action: to bring and to be the message
- *Meet* spiritual and physical human needs in the name of God
- *Be set apart* as holy to the Lord

---

1. In the world of the Hebrew Bible, people did not see or hear their gods. Priests were assigned to stand between a particular god and the people and represent the god to them. In some rituals, priests even wore the robes that were normally draped on the statue of the god in the temple. The people would learn about their god by observing the god's priest, who was to them the god in flesh. Although God was present in the tabernacle and later the temple, the priests of Israel were still responsible to communicate God's ways to his people.

    To better understand what it means to be a kingdom of priests, consider the responsibilities God gave to Israel's priests, how the Israelites viewed their role as priests, and how the early believers viewed their role. As you read the following passages, write down what God's priests were called to do and be.

The responsibilities God gave to Israel's priests: Teacher Offer Sacrifice for Sin Channel God's Blessing Healing Ministry of Divine Presence	Read: Malachi 2:7 Leviticus 9:6–24 2 Chronicles 2:37 Leviticus 13:1–8 Deuteronomy 18:6–8	Represent God by:
How the Israelites viewed their role as a kingdom of priests	Read: Deuteronomy 28:9–10; 1 Chronicles 16:8; Isaiah 2:1–5; 42:6–7; 43:10–12	Bring and be God's message by:
How the early believers viewed their role as a holy priesthood	Read: 1 Peter 2:4–17; Matthew 5:14–16; 28:19–20; Acts 13:47; Romans 12:1–2, 9–21; 1 Corinthians 11:1	Bring and be God's message by:

2. Read Deuteronomy 7:6 - 11; 26:17 - 19; 28:9; Leviticus 26:3 - 12; 2 Corinthians 7:1; and 1 Thessalonians 4:7.

   a. Which characteristic does God highly value in his people?

   b. Why do you think it is so important to him? (See Exodus 19:5 - 6; Leviticus 19:2; 20: 7 - 8, 26; Psalm 1:1 - 3; 5:4 - 5; 97:10.)

3. God commissioned Israel to be a holy (Hebrew, *kadosh*) nation, meaning "set apart" for a mission. They were to be distinct from the pagan nations around them by obeying God's commands regarding morality, devotion to him, compassion for those in need, purity, and even daily activities such as dress and diet. Being set apart would enable them to carry out the mission of displaying God to all nations through their words and actions. What did God command his people — his "kingdom of priests" — to wear, and for what purpose? (See Numbers 15:37 – 41; Deuteronomy 22:12.)

FOR GREATER UNDERSTANDING
Why Tassels?

In ancient times, the clothing people wore often revealed their identity and societal status. The hem and tassels (Hebrew, *tzitzit*) of the outer robe were particularly important, symbolizing the owner's identity and authority. Those in the upper class — nobility, kings, and princes — decorated their hems with tassels.

God wanted his people to stand out as unique among the nations — morally, socially, economically, and religiously — because of their obedience to him. By wearing tassels on their clothing, they wore what appeared to be robes of royalty. The tassels were a reminder to both Jews and Gentiles of their status as God's holy, chosen people.[11] *(cont.)*

God intended the tassels to be a constant reminder for his people to obey his commands—always. The tassels included a blue cord, which the Jewish people understood to be a reminder of their role as God's kingdom of priests who in every activity of life were to display him to the world and show how he wanted people to live. If they failed to obey, they would portray a flawed picture of the God who chose them to be his partners in redemption.

4. Although followers of Jesus are not commanded to wear tassels, we remain God's people, his royal priesthood, his holy nation (1 Peter 2:4 – 17). What did Jesus — and other biblical writers — continue to communicate about how we are to demonstrate what God is like and be the message God intends? (See John 14:15; James 1:22 – 25; 1 John 2:3.)

Reflection

Just as Israel's priests were to mediate and model the Lord to Israel, Israel was to mediate and model the Lord to the pagan world around them. As his kingdom of priests, they were called to demonstrate God's character by their words and their walk (lifestyle). By doing so they would fulfill God's promise to Abraham that all nations would be blessed by his descendants, and they would be faithful partners in making God's name known and bringing his redemptive grace to the ends of the earth.

Today, God continues to call a kingdom of priests consisting of people who believe in Jesus to demonstrate his character and make his name known to a world that does not know him. As God's kingdom of priests, those of us who follow Jesus are what is described in Matthew 5:14 – 16 as God's light to the world: "A town built on a hill cannot be hidden. Neither do people light a lamp and put it under a bowl. Instead they put it on its stand, and it gives light to everyone in the house. In the same way, let your light shine before others, that they may see your good deeds and glorify your Father in heaven."

To be God's light to the world, we must be obedient, distinctly righteous, and faithfully reflect the holiness to which we are called. God's intent was not that we would impact our world with brilliant, logical arguments — although these certainly have their place. Rather, our light shines and our message is understood through the language of a holy, faithful walk that displays God's character, love, values, and blessing by the way we live every day.

> In Romans 12:1 – 2, Paul urged his fellow believers not to conform to the ways of the world, but to *be* a holy, living sacrifice to God. In 12:9 – 21, he described in practical terms what that holy life — a life set apart for God's purpose — looks like. Describe in your own words what such a life looks like in your world.

To what extent do you see Jesus' followers today being God's kingdom of priests who draw other people to God?

Is it possible that the Christian community has increasingly less impact on the culture around us because our lives do not faithfully portray what we say we believe? Why or why not?

In which area(s) of life do you find it most challenging to be God's light and to display him accurately to the world around you? What makes this difficult for you?

Which step(s) will you take, starting now, to renew your commitment as a follower of Jesus to obey God fully and be who he calls you to be?

Memorize

> *You are the light of the world. A town built on a hill cannot be hidden. Neither do people light a lamp and put it under a bowl. Instead they put it on its stand, and it gives light to everyone in the house. In the same way, let your light shine before others, that they may see your good deeds and glorify your Father in heaven.*
>
> *Matthew 5:14–16*

Study 2 | Going to the "Other Side"

The Very Words of God

> *When the teachers of the law who were Pharisees saw him eating with the sinners and tax collectors, they asked his disciples: "Why does he eat with tax collectors and sinners?"*
>
> *On hearing this, Jesus said to them, "It is not the healthy who need a doctor, but the sick. I have not come to call the righteous, but sinners."*
>
> *Mark 2:16–17*

Bible Discovery

Fulfilling God's Mission to the Other Side

The Hebrew Bible declares the importance of avoiding sin and sinners. God hates sin, so we — his people — must also hate sin. The Torah clearly instructed God's people to walk in his ways and avoid everything that was "unclean" so that they would not be contaminated by sin or risk joining the company of sinners on the wrong path. At the same time God required holiness, he also gave his people the mission to be a light to all nations and display him to all people — even unclean, pagan sinners.

The tension between Israel's identity as a holy people and their mission as a light to a pagan world is understandable. They were to avoid being influenced by pagan practices and beliefs, yet they were to interact with pagan people so they might come to know Israel's God. How does one do both? Israel struggled to find the right balance. Sometimes they were too much like the nations around them; other times they were so dedicated to being holy that they insulated themselves from being a witness to people on the other side who desperately needed God.

The latter choice was particularly true when the Jewish exiles returned from Babylon after God punished them for their lack of holiness. Once again in the Promised Land, they were determined to be a more faithful kingdom of priests,[12] and they diligently applied God's revealed Word to the practical matters of daily life. Of course, not all Jews remained faithful to God, but those who did became good at wearing their tassels!

Although Israel often failed in carrying out the redemptive mission God gave them, they were not failures, and God did not give up on them. Jesus came to redeem his people from their sin and to restore the mission by personally carrying it out on Israel's behalf. Jesus, the Word in the flesh,[13] "became Israel with them" in order to make God known to all nations.

By his teaching and example, Jesus showed his disciples that holiness is not an end in itself. Rather, going to the other side is part of the mission! Going to the other side is part of what it means to obey God. Going to the other side to take back what belongs to God is part of what it means to do his will so that his kingdom reigns on earth as it does in heaven.

1. It would not be easy for Jesus' disciples to learn their role in going to the other side, yet Jesus was a faithful teacher. Consider how each of the following situations would have demonstrated to Jesus' disciples the need to step out of their comfort zone and engage with the other side.

   a. In Luke 19:5 – 10, Jesus was criticized for going into the house of a known sinner. In contrast, what was Jesus excited about, and what did it have to do with the mission God has given his people?

b. In Luke 15, the Pharisees criticized Jesus for eating with tax collectors and sinners. In response, Jesus told them a parable about a lost sheep, a lost coin, and a lost son. What did Jesus say that conveyed the importance of seeking the lost? (See Luke 15:5 – 7; 9 – 10; 22 – 24; 31 – 32.[14])

c. To ensure that his disciples really understood his desire for them to reach out into an unclean world, Jesus took them to Caesarea Philippi — one of the most decadent, pagan places in the region.[15] In the midst of flagrant evil, what did Jesus ask his disciples to affirm, and what did he say they were to do? (See Matthew 16:13 – 20.)

d. The Torah describes in detail what is clean and unclean (Leviticus 11 – 17; Numbers 19). Numbers 5:1 – 4 defined infectious skin diseases such as leprosy as unclean and required people who were so afflicted to live apart from God's community of people. What shocking thing did Jesus do to restore one of the culture's most pitiful and diseased individuals to God's community of people? What message did his action communicate? (See Matthew 8:1 – 3.)

FOR GREATER UNDERSTANDING
Capernaum: Known for Pursuing Righteousness

During his teaching ministry, Jesus lived in the village of Capernaum[16] on the north shore of the Sea of Galilee, about two and a half miles west of where the Jordan River enters the Sea. The village was founded around 150 BC, and as many as 1,200 people lived within its 225 acres. Its citizens were mainly fishermen, stonecutters, and farmers. In addition, the great trade route, *Via Maris,* passed by the village, so residents provided services to travelers on the Roman road. A Roman garrison and a customs house (where tax collectors worked) were also located there.

Capernaum was quite prosperous during Jesus' time, but perhaps more significant for his purposes were the people who lived there. Capernaum, along with the nearby towns of Bethsaida and Chorazin, formed the "gospel triangle," where the Jewish population was known for fervent obedience to God's commands in every area of life. In this part of Galilee, Jesus lived among a core community well-versed in the Hebrew Bible and dedicated to studying, interpreting, teaching, and obeying it.

THE FOURTH-CENTURY CAPERNAUM SYNAGOGUE

THE DARK, LOWER PORTION OF THE SYNAGOGUE WALL IS THE FOUNDATION OF THE FIRST-CENTURY CAPERNAUM SYNAGOGUE.

In the center of the village was the synagogue, the hub of religious life. The ruins of the synagogue where the gospel writers place Jesus and several events related to his ministry are believed to lie beneath the white limestone ruins of a fourth-century synagogue. A layer of black basalt cobblestones under the white limestone synagogue was obviously the floor of an earlier building and clearly dates to the first century or earlier. The plan and footprint of the first-century building is the same as the later synagogue, which consists of the main prayer hall and a large hall next to it believed to be the school.

If Jesus wanted holy, committed, faithful "priests" to carry on his mission, Capernaum would be the place to find them. In fact, the disciples Peter, Andrew, James, and John are mentioned as living in the village (although scholars believe that Peter and Andrew originally came from Bethsaida). In addition, Matthew the tax collector came from Capernaum. How would Jesus teach his faithful, God-fearing disciples to step out of their safe, clean community and take his gospel to the "other side"?

2. The pattern for many of Jesus' redemptive acts is found in the Hebrew Bible, including the storm on the Sea of Galilee when Jesus took his disciples by boat to the other side (Mark 4:35 – 41). Read the following passages of Scripture and consider how the Gospel writers framed the story of Jesus' venture to the "other side" known as the Decapolis in the context of Jonah's venture to the "other side" known as Nineveh.[17]

The Text	Jonah's Mission to Nineveh	Jesus' Mission to the Decapolis
2 Kings 14:25; Matthew 4:12–17	Jonah came from Galilee and began ministry there	Jesus came from Galilee and began ministry there[18]
Jonah 1:1–3; Luke 2:28–32	Jonah given a mission to bring God's message of repentance to the Gentile Ninevites	Jesus on a mission to bring good news of the kingdom to Gentiles and put God on display
Jonah 1:5; Mark 4:38	Jonah fell asleep in the ship	Jesus fell asleep in the boat
Jonah 1:4, 11; Mark 4:37	A terrible storm erupted with wind and waves	A terrible storm erupted with wind and waves
Jonah 1:6; Mark 4:38	Captain awakened Jonah and asked him to pray so they would not perish	Disciples awakened Jesus because they were afraid they would perish
Jonah 1:10, 16; Mark 4:41	Ship's sailors were terrified	Disciples were terrified
Jonah 1:15; Mark 4:39	After sailors threw Jonah overboard, sea became calm	Jesus rebuked the wind and waves, which became calm
Jonah 3:3; Mark 5:1–2	Jonah finally arrived at Nineveh	Jesus arrived on the "other side" at the Decapolis

The stories describe how Jonah and Jesus each fulfilled the mission of making God known to people on the other side, people who needed to be set free from bondage to the Evil One.

a. Why was Jonah — and by implication, Israel — unwilling or unable to be God's witness in the world?

b. Why do you think it was important for Jesus to be God's faithful witness to an unclean, pagan world?

THINK ABOUT IT

It is not easy for us to comprehend the strength of the disciples' aversion to going to the "other side." Bargil Pixner, a noted scholar on Galilee, has noted that in the Talmud and writings of the Church Fathers, the people of the Decapolis were thought to be descendants of the seven Canaanite nations Joshua and the Israelites drove out of the Promised Land.[19] These pagan nations worshiped Baal, sacrificed and ate pigs, and used sexual perversion and child sacrifice in their worship.[20] Apparently, the Jews considered the practices and values of the people of the Decapolis to be continuations of the idolatry and detestable practices of the Canaanites. We do not know how many Jews actually believed that the people of the Decapolis descended from the Canaanites, but the link between their blasphemous practices helps to establish the validity of this Jewish view.

3. Why is it significant that Mark's account of Jesus going to the other side to restore the demoniac to health (Mark 5:1 – 20) does not mention the disciples having a part, or even getting out of the boat? What do you think they did, and why?

Reflection

There is a rabbinic saying, "The word (of God) must become flesh," meaning that God intends people to be affected by his words when they see those words lived out in the lives of ordinary people. That was Israel's mission, and those of us who follow Jesus today also are challenged to become the word of God in flesh, revealing his true nature by the way we obey him in every area of life. We are his kingdom of priests, called to *bring* and to *be* God's message of restoration and hope in a fractured world.

In order to fulfill our mission, we must be willing to obey God and follow Jesus to the other side. People in Jesus' day were willing to fulfill the obedience part, but their fear of being corrupted led them to avoid the other side. Instead of taking God's kingdom to the other side, they sat in judgment, offering criticism and offensive names rather than hope and grace.

Yes, the other side is the kingdom of this world — the kingdom of darkness. It is unclean. It is threatening. But not one square inch of it belongs to the Evil One! It all belongs to the King of kings. We have the opportunity to go to the other side and take away from the Evil One what belongs to God — one situation, one relationship, one opportunity at a time — so that Satan's kingdom is diminished and the kingdom of our Messiah is extended.

> How badly do you want to obey Jesus' command to go to the other side and engage the chaos of our broken world so that God's will may be done?

> In what way(s) do you struggle to find the balance between obedient, holy living and engaging with your world to display the good news of the kingdom of God among people who are corrupted and enslaved by Satan?

> For what reasons do you hesitate going to the other side?

God gives each of us opportunities to go to the other side and bring God's reign into the lives of people in chaos. The other side may be found in classes in school or at work. It may be found on mission trips or when we pass homeless people in our cities. It may be found in people whose lifestyles we find repulsive or who practice or proclaim things we find offensive. In all of these places we must be willing to follow Jesus, get out of the boat, and put God on display.

> How do we do it? Consider the following: Psalm 145:8 – 9; Ezekiel 18:23; Matthew 25:35 – 45.

> Where are your opportunities to follow in the footsteps of Jesus and go to the other side?

> How far beyond your comfort zone will you go to be like him and make God known?

Memorize

> *Give praise to the LORD, proclaim his name; make known among the nations what he has done.*
>
> **1 Chronicles 16:8**

Study 3 | God's Kingdom Comes!

The Very Words of God

*The LORD will be king over the whole earth. On that day there will be
one LORD, and his name the only name.*

Zechariah 14:9

Bible Discovery

Jesus Binds the "Strong Man"

During the first century, the Jews suffered bitterly under the fist
of Imperial Rome. They knew God had controlled all things since
creation, and they knew they were God's chosen people, but they
were oppressed in a world dominated by evil, brutality, corruption,
and idolatry. They longed for Messiah (Hebrew, *moshiach*; English,
"anointed one"), the mighty, anointed king whom God had promised would appear to redeem his people and restore his kingdom on
earth.[21] They were eager for the Messiah to vanquish the wicked,
judge the nations, and establish his reign.

At least in the Jewish world, it seems the coming of God's kingdom
was on everyone's mind. Zealots expected to join their king in a
great war and meet their Roman overlords with violence. Essenes
saw themselves as "sons of light" and formed isolated communities
where they prayed for the day when God would destroy the "sons
of darkness." Pharisees believed that if God's people were righteous,
the king would establish his kingdom, so they called for repentance
and obedience. Even Jesus' disciples asked him "Lord, are you at this
time going to restore the kingdom to Israel?" (Acts 1:6).

Jesus came into the world bringing the good news that the kingdom
of heaven was at hand: the God of Israel had begun to act as King!
By his very life, death, and resurrection, Jesus embodied Israel's mission to make God's kingdom known so that all people in all nations
would acknowledge and submit to his reign.[22] His mission, which
was to establish a kingdom unlike the world's kingdoms, would be
misunderstood by the Jews. His mission would also bring him into

conflict with the kingdoms of this world — the kingdom of Rome and the kingdom of the Evil One. Let's consider some examples of how Jesus confronted Satan's kingdom and extended God's reign despite the Evil One's opposition.

DID YOU KNOW?

We tend to think of the kingdom of heaven as a place where we will spend eternity in fellowship with God. But when Jesus talked about God's kingdom, he was not referring to a place. In Hebrew, "kingdom" (*malkhut*) refers to the act of reigning as king, not to a geographic territory. So when Jesus declared that God's kingdom had come, he meant that God had begun to reign as king, or was "kinging." God reigns (his kingdom comes) as people obey him and serve him as their king. In contrast, if people are not obeying or serving the king, the king's reign is not established.

---

1. After John the Baptist was put in prison, Jesus moved to Capernaum, just a few miles from the palace of King Herod in Tiberias on the shore of the Sea of Galilee. From that time on, Jesus focused his ministry in Galilee, proclaiming the arrival of God's kingdom right under Herod's nose. He traveled throughout the region extending God's kingdom by teaching, calling sinners to repentance, and restoring *shalom* amidst the chaos of human suffering. One Sabbath, when he was teaching in the synagogue in Capernaum, another kingdom voiced its opposition. Read Mark 1:21 – 28 (also Luke 4:31 – 37) and consider the following questions.

   a. What impact did Jesus' teaching have on his audience, and how might their response indicate that God's kingdom was advancing and threatening Satan's kingdom?

b. How did this demon-possessed man respond to Jesus, and what were the demons most concerned about? What did they recognize as being different about Jesus?

c. Think back to our study of the storm on the Sea of Galilee when Jesus and his disciples went to take the news of God's kingdom to the other side. What do you think this man's outburst suggests about the impact of Jesus' teaching and the reign of God?

d. What powerful act did Jesus do for this man, and what was the result for the kingdom of the Evil One? For the kingdom of God?

e. How did onlookers respond after Jesus freed this man from bondage to the kingdom of Satan?

2. In another instance, people brought to Jesus a demon-possessed man who could not speak or see. In which two ways did people respond when Jesus healed the man and set him free from bondage to the Evil One, and what conflict did their responses highlight? (See Matthew 12:22 – 24; Luke 11:14 – 16.)

DATA FILE
Who Has Power Over Demons?

According to Jewish tradition, demons were evil spiritual powers who could influence and even control people by "possessing" them. It was believed that such spirits could cause bodily diseases such as those exhibited by the man in the Matthew 12:22 – 29 story, mental disorder,[23] violent actions,[24] and even direct rebellion against God.[25] When Jesus drove away the demon and healed the man, certain Pharisees questioned the source of Jesus' amazing power.

The Pharisees believed that God empowered people to do mighty works and also recognized the power of "magic" — the use of spiritual forces to affect present circumstances. By saying that Jesus was casting out demons by the power of *Beelzebub*,[26] they were saying that his power came from Satan, the prince of darkness himself! The Gospel writers do not tell us whether it was Jesus' great power, the way he cast out demons, or what he taught that led some Jewish religious leaders to question whether this miracle was God's doing. It's interesting that Jesus reminded his detractors that some of their own were so devoted to the kingdom of heaven that God enabled them to bring his power against the Evil One and drive out demons too.

3. Notice how Jesus refuted the challenge to his power and authority to cast out demons. (See Matthew 12:25 – 28; Luke 11:17 – 20.)

   a. In terms of Jesus' mission and teaching, why was it important that he focus his response in terms of the conflict between the kingdom of heaven and the kingdom of Satan?

   b. What conclusions did Jesus want his audience to reach about himself and the kingdom of God as a result of casting out the demon and restoring the man to health?

4. Jesus continued his explanation (Matthew 12:29; Luke 11:21 – 22) with the image of entering a strong man's house, which his audience would have recognized as a metaphor for Satan's kingdom, and taking away his possessions.

   a. Why is it significant that Jesus was able to bind or tie up the strong man (meaning the Evil One) and rob him (in this case, take away from Satan's kingdom the demon-possessed man)?

b. What was Jesus revealing about the power of God's kingdom and what was in store for the future of Satan's kingdom?

FOR GREATER UNDERSTANDING
How Does God Reign?

When God sent Moses to free the Israelites—Abraham's enslaved descendants—from Egypt, he established a partnership in which they would be his kingdom of priests who would demonstrate to the entire world that he is Lord. In Jewish thought, this dramatic redemption initiated the kingdom of heaven, or God's reign on earth. That kingdom is identified by three elements:

First, the kingdom began when God dramatically confronted Egyptian gods and the kingdom of the Evil One and his demons[27] by bringing the ten plagues on the Egyptians. Egyptian magicians who served the demonic underworld were the first to recognize the superiority of God's power—what they called "the finger of God."[28] That power crushed the power of the gods of Egypt and redeemed Israel from bondage.

The second element is when people recognize God's redeeming power and call him not just Lord of all, but *their* Lord. After God's people saw the power of his little finger setting them free, they danced before him, called him their Lord, and sang that he reigns forever.[29] If the Lord is reigning, he is their King.

The third element is evident when God's people obey him and, by doing so, extend his reign on earth. At Mount Sinai, God gave Israel the mission to be his kingdom of priests and said they would be that kingdom *if* they would obey him fully and keep his covenant.[30] He had redeemed them by his grace and power. They had responded by calling him Lord. Now they must obey him in word and deed and thus put God on display so that all the world would know him as he truly is and see that his kingdom reigns! That is how God's kingdom comes!

Reflection

Jesus came not only to redeem humanity but to create a community of people, saved by grace through faith, who bring *shalom* to the sin and chaos around them — through submitting to God's will and thereby extending his reign. It is far too easy for Jesus' followers today to trivialize our disobedience by using the excuse that we still have a sinful nature. Although that is theologically correct, it does not change the fact that faith in Jesus means we accept him as our Savior and King, submit to him as Lord, and extend his reign by obeying him.

Our calling is to be disciples[31] who walk as Jesus walked and, by his presence in the person of his Spirit who enables us to overcome temptation,[32] make the reign of God a reality in our lives and in one small part of God's world. Every time we recite the prayer Jesus taught his disciples, "your kingdom come, your will be done,"[33] it reminds us that God's kingdom comes as we obey his will and bring his reign into our lives.

Lois Tverberg expresses this well:

> Believing in Christ is not about facts *per se,* but about believing in Jesus' authority to reign over God's kingdom. It means that you see his teachings as law, and that you realize that all of humanity is ultimately answerable to him. It implies that you've put yourself under his reign, and aim to follow his commands. Listen to John 3:36 with this in mind:
>
> "He who believes in the Son has eternal life; but he who does not obey the Son will not see life, but the wrath of God abides on him."
>
> Notice how "believing" is put in parallel with "obeying." This seems strange, doesn't it? But if "belief" is really about believing in Christ's sovereign authority, of course it means that one obeys what he says.[34]

It would be so easy to simply "catalogue" what you've learned about the kingdom of heaven during this session rather than acting on it. But God longs for human partners who are committed to obeying his every command so that his kingdom — his reign — advances and his *shalom* shatters the chaos that keeps people in bondage.

> How deeply, how passionately, are you committed to obey the commands of Jesus? To establish the Lord as your King?

> What new understanding do you now have of Jesus' commands in Matthew 22:37 – 39 and John 14:15?

> How willing are you to make changes in your life in order to make his ways your ways and to love him with all your heart, soul, and mind? What are some of these changes in attitude, action, faithfulness, and words?

> In what ways might the world's perception of God and his kingdom change if Jesus-followers today were totally devoted to God and his reign and refused to compromise on obeying him?

POINT TO PONDER

Jesus' proclamation and demonstration of the kingdom of heaven apparently startled his audience. They were so amazed by his power and apparent authority that they were concerned he was out of his normal mind or under the influence of the Evil One. When we demonstrate the kingdom of heaven as God intends it to be, we must realize that people may be offended or become angry.

In Western culture, which at times has been significantly influenced by followers of Jesus, it is tempting to think that living out the kingdom of heaven means being a "good citizen" of the culture. While that is sometimes true, the assumption that what is "normal" in society resembles the kingdom of heaven is often flawed. The kingdom of heaven, the reign of God, is where his will is obeyed and where *shalom* is found.

Shalom is not about economic prosperity, political power, pleasure, or leisure. *Shalom* is where God defeats the chaos of evil, whether it be human suffering, broken relationships, materialism, or the mad pursuit of pleasure. It is where the hungry are fed, the thirsty receive drink, the homeless find shelter, the naked are clothed, the sick are comforted, and the lonely become part of a community. In a self-centered, self-sufficient culture, having this vision of God's kingdom may label you out of your mind or worse.

Memorize

Not everyone who says to me, "Lord, Lord," will enter the kingdom of heaven, but only the one who does the will of my Father who is in heaven.

Matthew 7:21

DECAPOLIS: THE OTHER SIDE – JESUS AND THE MAN FROM THE TOMBS

It's easy for us to miss the significance of Jesus' command for his disciples to join him and "go over to the other side."[1] The "other side" was where the Gentiles lived, where God's reign was opposed by the kingdom of the Evil One. In Jesus' day faithful, God-fearing Jews would have nothing to do with the other side. In their eyes, the people of the other side had to be avoided because of their self-serving, sinful lifestyles or their contact with tombs, idols, and unclean animals. Faithful Jews would not even enter a Gentile's house lest they become ritually impure or tempted to engage in practices God had forbidden in Torah.

Yet in clear view across the Sea of Galilee from Capernaum, where Jesus lived during his teaching ministry, was Hippos (Susita to the Jews), a city of the Decapolis. There people valued the Hellenistic worldview dominated by the pursuit of power, pleasure, wealth, fame, accomplishment, and leisure. Their lifestyle and especially their religious practices violated God's prohibitions against idolatry, adultery, and bloodshed. The other side of the Sea of Galilee was a spiritually dark place in bondage to the Evil One. It represented everything God's people on the northern side of the Sea of Galilee avoided.

When Jesus announced to his disciples that he was going to the other side and wanted them to join him, they likely were startled. Even so, his command was predictable. The disciples knew the Scriptures and were well aware of the Evil One's mission to destroy

God's *shalom* and maintain chaos on earth. They knew God had a plan to take back — to redeem — his sin-scarred creation. They knew that God would not bring about redemption by the power of his command alone, but in partnership with the human race that initially brought chaos into the world. And they knew that they were part of that plan because God had chosen Israel to be his people and had given them the mission of being his kingdom of holy priests who would display him to all nations.

God's people had struggled to fulfill their role of being spiritual light amidst the darkness of evil. They often became so engaged in sin that they became like the people to whom God had called them to be witnesses, and God disciplined them severely. At other times they were so concerned about not presenting a flawed picture of God that they isolated themselves from the world around them. At the time of Jesus, the Jewish people in Galilee had so devoted themselves to holiness that they no longer engaged with the people they were commanded to reach. They expected God to destroy the Gentiles rather than to redeem them!

But Jesus was not confused about his mission. God's desire to redeem all people had not diminished. When Jesus instructed his disciples to go to the other side, he was continuing the mission God had given Israel from the time of Abraham. Jesus clearly intended for his disciples to go to "the ends of the earth"[2] and be his witnesses to all nations. He would not stay in Capernaum and preach against the evil on the far side of the Sea of Galilee. He had come to save the world, not to condemn it.[3] He had come to defeat the power and authority of the Evil One. So he went boldly to the other side to reclaim the life of a man in bondage, to restore God's *shalom* to a man filled with a host of demons.

Opening Thoughts (3 minutes)

The Very Words of God

> *That day when evening came, he [Jesus] said to his disciples, "Let us go over to the other side."*
>
> **Mark 4:35**

Think About It

God's people who seek to represent and display the kingdom of God in their world have always encountered some degree of opposition. What are some examples of opposition to God's kingdom that are evident in our own culture?

What are some of the ways we tend to respond to people who live in opposition to what we understand God's kingdom to be?

In what ways do our responses accurately reflect and advance God's kingdom, and in what ways might they diminish it?

Video Notes (30 minutes)

The kingdom of the "other side"

The worldview of the Roman gospel

The values of Hellenism

The kingdom of God

    Rescue and restore the marginalized

Jesus takes back what the "strong man" has stolen

Jesus goes to the "other side"

Lessons from the "other side"

Video Discussion (8 minutes)

1. Look at the maps of the Roman Empire, the Decapolis, and Galilee at the time of Jesus. Note particularly the small "triangle" of Capernaum, Chorazin, and Bethsaida where many obedient, faithful Jews lived.

   a. As you viewed the ruins of Hippos — the smallest city of the Decapolis — and learned a bit about its history, people, and culture, what did you realize about how powerful an influence the gospel of Rome had on the world of Jesus' day?

THE "KINGDOM" OF THE ROMAN WORLD

b. What chance would you give for God's message of redemption, going out from the small communities of Galilee, to have a significant influence on the Roman world? Why?

2. How does the idea of opposing kingdoms — the kingdom of God and the evil kingdom of the "strong man" — each with its own worldview and value system, help you to better understand the mission and message of Jesus? The mission and message of followers of Jesus today?

3. What value would the demoniac have had in the eyes of people who lived according to the worldview of Hippos? In the minds of God-fearing Jews who lived in Galilee?

What does the fact that Jesus went to the other side to release and heal a man who was utterly unacceptable and shunned by everyone — Jews as well as Gentiles — tell you about God's love and desire to redeem and restore marginalized people?

If we desire to join God in his plan to take back his lost children from the strong man and restore them to relationship with their heavenly Father, what changes might we need to make in our attitudes and willingness to embrace people who may appear to be beyond redemption? And who are some of these people?

FOR GREATER UNDERSTANDING
Restored to the Father's House

God's plan for restoring *shalom* to his broken world includes rescuing alienated sinners and bringing them back into relationship with him. To understand what being restored to relationship with God our Father entails, we need to consider the patriarchal family structure as practiced in ancient Israel.

At that time, life centered around the extended family or household, which was called the "father's house" (Hebrew, *beth ab*). The father, or patriarch, controlled all family resources for the purpose of protecting and caring for each family member. If a member became marginalized due to oppression, capture by enemies, poverty, or bad choices, the patriarch assumed responsibility — and would spare no effort or expense — to restore that person to the *beth ab*.

Abraham recognized his role as God's partner in restoring *shalom* to those who were alienated from God. He had a mission to bless all people and nations by displaying God in such a way that those who were estranged from God would come to know him and experience restoration to the *beth ab*. Jesus came to continue that mission and gave his life to restore all of God's lost children to the *beth ab*. Jesus has passed on to everyone who follows him the mission of displaying God accurately so that his lost children may be restored.

4. Imagine for a minute what the whole experience of going to the other side with Jesus might have been like for his disciples. They had lived their lives near the Sea of Galilee with the other side clearly in view, yet had never ventured over there.

    a. In what ways had Jesus' actions challenged their view of who he was and what it meant to obey God and display him to the world around them?

    b. What impact do you think the experience with Jesus and the demoniac might have had on them? What impact does it have on you?

Small Group Bible Discovery and Discussion (14 minutes)

Jesus Plunders the Strong Man's House

When Jesus said to his disciples, "Let us go over to the other side," he was not inviting them on a relaxing sunset cruise. Jesus was on the attack! He was going there to wage war and plunder the enemy in his own house. He knew the Evil One would not relinquish his kingdom, those who were in bondage to him, without a fight.

When Jesus came to earth to live out the message of the kingdom of God, conflict between the kingdom of heaven and the kingdom of this world escalated. The Evil One sought to stop the pagan world — Caesar's world — from hearing the message of redemption and restoration that Jesus brought to all people. So when Jesus and his disciples ventured to the other side, they would face the worst kind of chaos imaginable.

But the kingdom of God had come. It would not be stopped. Jesus would complete his mission, and his disciples and everyone who walks as Jesus walked would continue it.

1. The gospel of Mark records what Jesus and his disciples encountered when they went to the "other side," meaning the Decapolis, on the eastern shore of the Sea of Galilee. Read Mark 5:1 – 8 as background and discuss the following:

   a. When Jesus reached the shore, who came running to meet him, and what was the tone of their encounter? What contrasts do you see in their interaction?

   b. It seems that the evil forces portrayed in this passage go far beyond the demons Jesus had driven away previously, as if the power and influence of evil was greater among the pagans of the Decapolis than among the Jews of Galilee. How powerful were the evil spirits, and how completely had they controlled the possessed man?

   c. What did the demons try to do when they encountered Jesus, and how well did they succeed?

DID YOU KNOW?

The demon-possessed man addressed Jesus as the "Son of the Most High God," a phrase that strongly suggests he was a Gentile because they commonly identified the Jewish God as "God Most High." This phrase also indicates a pagan context in which polytheism was practiced because Jesus is called the Son of the "Most High" God as if there were other gods as well. This phrase is rarely used in the Hebrew Text (Psalm 7:10; 78:35).

2. Jesus knew that the confrontation on the other side was not simply between him and the possessed man: it was a confrontation with the Evil One, a confrontation between the kingdom of heaven and the kingdom of this world. But Jesus had power to bind the "strong man" and had done so on previous occasions, so there was no doubt as to how the confrontation would end. (See Mark 5:7 – 10.)

    a. What information did Jesus demand from the demons?

    b. What did the demons do and say that indicated they recognized Jesus' authority and feared that the confrontation would end badly for them?

FOR GREATER UNDERSTANDING
The Power of a Name

Imagine the evil power the legion of demons exerted over the possessed man. He was totally under the Evil One's control. His every thought was only evil all the time.[4] The man recognized Jesus and ran to him, seeking to control him. The demons then attempted to control Jesus by using his name, believing that would give them influence or control over his divine powers.

When the demons said, "In God's name don't torture me," they were giving Jesus a command! "I adjure you, don't torture me" (NRSV), they demanded. *Adjure*—the word used in casting out demons—is translated from the ancient Greek, *orkidzo*, from which we get the English word *exorcism*. The demons actually tried to exorcise Jesus out of their region!

In Jewish culture, people believed that knowing the name of a demon or evil power was essential in order to exorcise or influence a spirit. So Jesus turned the tables on the demons when he forced them to reveal their name, Legion, and with that knowledge expelled them. The fact that the demons revealed their name to Jesus shows that they understood the superiority of his power and authority.

3. Despite their attempts, the demons could not resist Jesus' command to come out of the man from the tombs, yet they still tried to maintain control and find a way to get Jesus to leave them alone. (See Mark 5:7 – 13; also Luke 8:31.)

   a. Where did the demons fear that Jesus would send them[5], and why might they have thought the pigs to be a "safe" place to escape Jesus' influence?

b. The Gospels do not comment on whether Jesus sent the
    pigs into the sea — a symbol of the abyss — or whether
    the demons drowned as a result of their normal, life-
    destroying activity. In any case, what does this turn of
    events reveal about Jesus' power over the Evil One and
    his demons?

4. The encounter between Jesus and the Legion of demons that
    possessed the man from the tombs created quite a spectacle
    for the local people. (See Mark 5:14 – 17.)

    a. What kind of a picture of life in God's kingdom did Jesus
        display through these events, and how did that picture
        differ from the life people in the Decapolis knew?

    b. How might life under the influence of the kingdom of
        God have appeared to them, and why do you think they
        responded in fear?

5. We can be thankful that these demons no longer wander
    God's earth seeking a new "host" to carry out their evil intent.
    From the beginning of his ministry, Jesus actively encountered
    the power of the Evil One. He has bound the strong man.
    The forces of evil are held in check by the power of God that
    brings *shalom* out of chaos. It is up to those of us who follow

Jesus to recognize that serving our King and faithfully accomplishing his will on earth will interfere with the power of evil and plunder the kingdom of this world. What assurance do we have that the power of God and his Word is greater than the power of the Evil One? (See Matthew 4:1–11.)

DATA FILE
Where Did Jesus Cast Out the Legion of Demons?

It is fascinating to try to locate places where significant events recorded in the Bible took place, and it is particularly helpful, although not necessary, in picturing this story. For some reason the ancient texts provide three locations for this event: Gerasa, Gergesa, and Gadara (Gerasene, Gergesene, and Gadarene). I will not discuss all the reasons why, but I support the traditional site, Kursi, which is likely a derivative of Gergesa, that lies along the Sea of Galilee just north of Susita (or Hippos).[6]

Only one location on the eastern side of the Sea of Galilee fits Luke's description of the herd of pigs rushing down a steep bank into the lake, and that is Kursi. Tradition supporting this location is ancient and strong, including that of the church father, Origen. Furthermore, we know the demoniac lived in tombs and there is evidence of tombs in this area.

This study was filmed at Susita, as it is the closest *polis* or free city state (about three miles away) to Kursi, and likely the place from which people came to see Jesus after he cast the demons into the herd of pigs. The city states of Gadara and Gerasa are about ten and twenty-five miles away, respectively, and more than 1,500 feet higher in altitude. Even at a dead run, it would take a trained athlete hours to travel from the site of Jesus' miracle by the Sea of Galilee to either of these cities and back to Jesus before he returned to Galilee. Given the nature of pigs, it is unlikely that their owners lived such a great distance away.   *(cont.)*

It is interesting to note that Jewish tradition connects the area near Kursi and Susita with the Gergeshites, a nation that Joshua expelled from the Promised Land. In this story, Jesus expelled evil spirits from the demoniac and the townspeople attempted to expel Jesus from their land. Repeating the theme of expelling is a very Jewish way to frame the story.

Faith Lesson (4 minutes)

Many visitors to Galilee are amazed by how close Jesus' area of ministry was to the Decapolis. Although Jesus did not focus his ministry on the Gentiles, he did not avoid the people living in spiritual darkness.[7] He went to them and pierced the darkness with the light of God's message. Today, Jesus wants all who follow him to imitate his example in confronting spiritual darkness. He calls us to commit ourselves to God as our King and to faithfully accomplish his will on earth — thereby extending the kingdom of heaven and diminishing the kingdom of the Evil One.

The power of Satan and his demons can seem frightening and overwhelming to us. It is easy for us to isolate ourselves in safe communities and let the outside world destroy itself. But Jesus modeled another way. He left the familiarity of his community and confronted evil on its own turf. He took on the kingdom of the Evil One. He bound the strong man and wants his followers to join him in plundering his kingdom — in taking back what rightfully belongs to God but is held in bondage by the Evil One.

God's restoration begins in the territory the Evil One has stolen from God. Whether the chaos is seen in human suffering, broken relationships, materialism, or the mad pursuit of pleasure, the *shalom* of God's kingdom breaks out whenever God's people go to the other side and live out the kingdom of God. When the hungry are fed, the thirsty receive drink, the homeless find shelter, the naked are clothed, the sick are comforted, the oppressed are lifted up, and the lonely become part of a community, Satan's power is defeated and God's kingdom comes.

So do you want to be part of something really big? Then be God's instrument in extending his kingdom!

1. Almost daily, I present to my students two challenges. Will you accept these challenges as well?

   • The first challenge is to obey God in all things and reclaim one situation, one moment, one inch of territory from the Evil One whenever the opportunity arises. Through faith in Jesus, God can bind the Evil One and cause his kingdom to come as his will is done!

   • The second challenge is to never give away anything that is part of God's kingdom. Every time we succumb to the will of the Evil One instead of the Lord, we give away one situation, one moment, one small piece of the kingdom of heaven.

2. If you hesitate in going to the other side, wherever that may be, what is hindering you from relying on God's superior power to defeat evil and accomplish his will?

Closing (1 minute)

Read Isaiah 9:2 aloud together: "The people walking in darkness have seen a great light; on those living in the land of deep darkness a light has dawned."

Then pray, thanking God for his unfailing love for every human he has created. Praise him for sending Jesus, his redeeming light, to make his kingdom known to all of us who have lived in the darkness of Satan's kingdom. Pray for love, courage, and faithfulness in displaying God's kingdom and fulfilling our mission to be God's light to the dark places in our world.

Memorize

> *The people walking in darkness have seen a great light; on those living in the land of deep darkness a light has dawned.*
>
> *Isaiah 9:2*

The Kingdom of Heaven Advances: Reclaiming What Belongs to God

In-Depth Personal Study Sessions

Study 1 | God Desires All People to Come to Him

The Very Words of God

> *This is what the* LORD *says: "As when juice is still found in a cluster of grapes and people say, 'Don't destroy it, there is still a blessing in it,' so will I do in behalf of my servants."*
>
> Isaiah 65:8

Bible Discovery

Jesus Cares about Every Person Outside of God's "House"

When Jesus took his disciples to the other side and freed the demoniac from Satan's bondage, he validated the truth that all human beings — pagans as well as those who obey God — are created in God's image. This concept appears early in Scripture[8] and was a central theme in Jewish thought during Jesus' time. Certainly sin has corrupted that image, yet all of humanity somehow bears the image of the Creator.

In Jewish thought, it is possible to encounter the divine within human relationships, to see the face of God in one's neighbor. No matter how corrupted that person may be, he or she still reflects — however dimly — the image of God. The biblical concept of creation in the divine image leads to the awe-inspiring insight that the most holy being a person will ever encounter in life (aside from God himself) is a fellow human being.

The idea of all people having inestimable worth because they are made in God's image was foreign to the Hellenistic culture of the

Greeks and Romans. In that world, worth was assigned according to beauty, accomplishment, wealth, power, intellect, and social status. In that world the demoniac had no value. He was a zero. His whole community saw him as absolutely worthless because he contributed nothing, accomplished nothing, owned nothing, had no social skills, and certainly had no beauty.

The demoniac didn't fare much better in the eyes of faithful Jews who lived by the Sea of Galilee. To them, the demoniac was unap-proachably unclean. He had to be avoided and shunned lest his uncleanness corrupt the purity of God's people. Yes, the Jews were right to pursue purity as God had commanded them. But they missed the point that they were to be holy and righteous *in order to* display God's love and redeeming power to people who were exactly like this man!

In contrast, Jesus recognized much more in the demoniac than his uncleanness. Jesus saw him as one of God's lost children trapped under the dominion of the power of evil. He had left heaven for people exactly like this poor, hopeless man. To Jesus, even the most unclean sinner is a child of God created in his image and thereby worthy of love and redemption. This man would not die, unnoticed, in a tomb with no one to care or mourn for him. Jesus would spare no effort to restore this man to the *beth ab*. He invited his disciples to join him and, by action, commanded them to be like him: to seek out the unclean and bring God's redemptive power to bear on the kingdom of evil. His desire for his disciples has not changed.

1. Mark 5:1 – 5 presents a vivid picture of the kind of man Jesus and his disciples faced when they reached the other side.

    a. Try to imagine what it was like for Jesus' disciples, who already had a frightening experience with evil as they crossed the Sea of Galilee (and a terrifying realization of the divine power of Jesus when he silenced the storm), to encounter the man possessed by a legion of demons. They may have heard his screams as they approached the shore and seen the tombs from which he ran toward them. He was naked, dirty, and likely covered with ooz-ing sores and open wounds. He confirmed every image they had about the Gentiles' unclean world. As they watched Jesus reach out to this desperately unclean man, what do you think they realized about fulfilling their mission to put God on display in a pagan world? Why was it important for Jesus to *take* them into this world, not just *send* them into it?

b. What do you realize about Jesus' love and commitment to his mission based on the depth of compassion and care he expressed toward this man? In what ways does his example show you how to fulfill the mission?

FOR GREATER UNDERSTANDING
The Pursuit of Holiness: Avoiding the Unclean

The Torah is clear that God's desire for Israel to display him to the nations in all his holiness required that his people avoid all that was unclean. Uncleanness included some skin disorders, bodily discharge, dead bodies, and certain animals.[9] These commands provided extensive rituals to remove the defilement of contact with the unclean[10] and made Israel distinct from the pagans to whom they were to be witnesses.

For example, commands to avoid contact with dead bodies and anything touched by death distinguished them from the Egyptian culture in which the Hebrews had lived for generations. Life in Egypt revolved around death, pyramids, tombs, mummification, funerary temples, rituals, and the *Book of the Dead*. So God's chosen people were to have no contact with death in any way, which separated them from their past in Egypt and made them unique in their display of the God of the universe.

Leviticus 11 lists certain unclean animals including pigs, which most of Israel's pagan neighbors ate. Other passages, such as Amos 7:17 (ESV), Isaiah 30:22, and Leviticus 18:27–28, list other things that were considered to be ritually impure. These included idols of any kind and even the Promised Land itself if Israel failed to obey God.

The concept that pagan lands were unclean was central to Jewish thought during Jesus' day. Pagan lands were filled with ritual impurities of every kind — unclean animals, multitudes of gods and idols, and sexual practices including ritual prostitution. The uncleanness was so extreme that Jews of Jesus' day shunned the ritually impure with great intensity.

2. Jesus left the glorious holiness of heaven to be born in a shepherd's cave. Why did he come to earth? (See Matthew 9:10 – 13; Luke 19:10; John 3:16 – 17; 9:5; 18:37; 1 Timothy 2:3 – 6.)

    a. What do Jesus' reasons for coming reveal about how highly he values even the most undesirable, seemingly hopeless people?

    b. How highly do you think God values every person — including sinners of all types — and what was Jesus willing to endure in order to restore them all to the Father's House? (See Isaiah 53:3 – 5, 10 – 12; Luke 15:4 – 10, 22 – 24.)

3. What did Simon prophesy about the infant Jesus at the temple in Jerusalem that shows God's love for all people, Jews as well as Gentiles? (See Luke 2:28 – 32.)

4. The ancient sages or rabbis of Jesus' time used a teaching technique called *midrash* to illustrate and explain Bible texts. One type of *midrash* explains one story by its similarity to an earlier story. To better understand God's desire to seek all unclean sinners and restore them to himself, consider how the disobedience of God's people (Isaiah 65:1 – 9) parallels the condition of the Gentile demoniac (Mark 5:1 – 20).

Question	Israel in Isaiah 65	The Demoniac in Mark 5
To whom does God make himself known?	v. 1 To people who did not seek him or ask for him	vv. 1 – 2
Which metaphors did Isaiah use to describe the ways they displayed their unfaithfulness?	v. 4 sit among the graves; spend the night keeping secret vigil[11]; eat the flesh of pigs	vv. 3 – 7, 11
What metaphor does Isaiah use to describe God's love for his unfaithful people?	v. 8 a small amount of juice in a cluster of grapes (he still finds value in them)	vv. 8, 12 – 15, 18 – 20

5. After the demoniac was healed and restored to his rightful place in God's kingdom (*beth ab*), Jesus gave him an assignment: "Go home to your own people and tell them how much the Lord has done for you, and how he has had mercy on you" (Mark 5:19).

a. In what ways were each of us, like the demoniac, lost
    until we placed our faith in Jesus as Lord and Savior and
    by obedience allowed him to reign as our King?
    (See Ephesians 2:1 – 7.)

b. What assignment has God given to each of us?
    (See Ephesians 2:10.)

Reflection

After being freed from bondage to the Evil One, the man from the
tombs eagerly desired to follow Jesus and begged to go with him.
We can almost imagine the disciples cringing, thinking, *This man
came out of a tomb! He is unclean! Not in my boat!*

But Jesus had other plans for his long-lost child. He had made a broken man whole, and the kingdom of heaven was breaking out into
new territory. So Jesus gave the man from the tombs a mission, and
he joined the ranks of many people whom God has rescued from
Satan's kingdom and then used in mighty ways to extend the kingdom of heaven. Consider Tamar the Canaanite (Genesis 38; Matthew
1:3), Rahab the prostitute (Joshua 2, 6; Matthew 1:5), and Ruth the
Moabite (Ruth 1 – 4; Matthew 1:5).

We are no different. We may not look as hopeless and disgusting
as the man from the tombs, yet we also were living in "tombs" as
unclean people in a sinful world. And Jesus saw us as God's trea-
sured possession and came from heaven into our unclean world to
bind the strong man and restore us to his kingdom.

Without such mercy demonstrated to us that set us free from bondage to the Evil One, where would we be? How different would life be for you today if Jesus had not restored you to relationship with him?

Isaiah 45:20 – 24 is God's invitation for every captive of Satan's kingdom to turn to God and be saved. "Gather together and come;" God calls, "assemble, you fugitives from the nations" (v. 20).

How might we communicate to people in our world, through our actions and words, the invitation God presents in this passage — that he alone is God, that he wants to save them, and that he is the way to experience righteousness?

God's desire to restore his lost children is so intense that he will do whatever it takes to rescue and restore just one person — even if he is bound by a legion of demons and is living in a tomb. He calls all who call him Lord and King to join him in that mission.

In which practical ways can we demonstrate the same kind of love to people around us that Jesus demonstrated to the man in the tombs?

Memorize

As Jesus was getting into the boat, the man who had been demon-possessed begged to go with him. Jesus did not let him, but said, "Go home to your own people and tell them how much the Lord has done for you, and how he has had mercy on you." So the man went away and began to tell in the Decapolis how much Jesus had done for him. And all the people were amazed.

Mark 5:18 – 20

Study 2 | Advancing God's Kingdom into Enemy Territory

The Very Words of God

Finally, be strong in the Lord and in his mighty power. Put on the full armor of God, so that you can take your stand against the devil's schemes. For our struggle is not against flesh and blood, but against the rulers, against the authorities, against the powers of this dark world and against the spiritual forces of evil in the heavenly realms. Therefore put on the full armor of God, so that when the day of evil comes, you may be able to stand your ground, and after you have done everything, to stand.

Ephesians 6:10 – 13

Bible Discovery

Battle Plan for Extending God's Reign

The Evil One — Satan — and a host of evil spirits work constantly to defile and destroy God's creation. The kingdom of the Evil One entices all of humanity to choose its own way — its own pleasure, power, and prosperity — and to refuse to live as God intends and commands. That kingdom is cunning, powerful, and persistent. It glories in everything God prohibits and steals the life from those it holds in bondage.

Jesus came to earth as the Anointed One, the Christ, to bring the kingdom of heaven — that is, to extend God's reign into territory the Evil One has claimed for himself and to reclaim every person the enemy has stolen. But the Evil One doesn't give up easily. He is intent on using his substantial power to sabotage the coming of the kingdom of heaven. He will not relinquish one square inch of his kingdom without a fight. Only the power of God as exercised by the community of God's people can overcome the Evil One's destructive power.

Throughout history, God's people have battled the forces of the Evil One by doing God's will and thereby expanding his reign. When we accept Jesus as our King and submit to his reign in our lives,[12] we join that battle. The mission of Israel as demonstrated by Jesus continues today whenever the community of Jesus does God's will so that his healing, life-giving kingdom reigns. We will certainly face interference from the Evil One, who hates God and everyone who submits to Jesus as Lord and obeys him faithfully. We should not be surprised by fierce confrontation between these powerful, opposing kingdoms. Nor should we fear the conflict because Jesus has bound the strong man.

1. When Jesus reached the shore of the other side, the man from the tombs ran toward him. Which two opposing postures did the man assume, and what does this suggest about the nature of their encounter? (See Mark 5:6 – 8.)

THINK ABOUT IT
The Power of the Kingdom of This World: The Tenth Legion — Legio Fretensis

The demons Jesus cast out from the demoniac were named *Legion*, which is also the title for a complete unit of six thousand soldiers in the Roman army. In fact, Rome's Tenth Legion was likely based in the Decapolis near the Sea of Galilee in the region where these events took place. Readers of Mark's account would have inferred from the demons' name that the kingdoms of this world — especially Imperial Rome that was intoxicated with idolatry, adultery, and bloodshed — were under the control of the Evil One. This would be especially true for believers in Rome, for whom Mark likely wrote this gospel.

The power of the Tenth Legion was legendary. It was organized by Augustus Caesar in 41 BC to fight against Mark Antony in the civil war that ended the Roman Republic. *Fretensis* means "sea strait" because of the legion's famous victory at the Strait of Messina in 36 BC. Then, in 31 BC, the legion fought in the sea battle of Actium that marked Octavian's rise to power. Later, Octavian was named Augustus and deified, so it is no exaggeration to say that in the eyes of the Roman world this legion made Caesar Augustus Lord and God.

Archaeological evidence found in Caesarea shows that the legion was based in Judea during the reign of Herod the Great (37 – 4 BC) and was active in Galilee when Jesus taught in Capernaum. Later stationed in Syria, the legion put down the Jewish revolt immediately following Herod's death. This legion's symbols were the bull, a ship, and a fierce boar with great tusks. Its patron god was Neptune.

STANDARD OF THE TENTH ROMAN LEGION

© Zev Radovan, BiblelandPictures.com

It is fascinating to consider that Jesus, the Son of God, was born and was bringing the good news that God's kingdom had come at the same time the adopted son of Julius, the so-called "Son of God," was declaring Rome's good news that he was Lord and God. It heightens for us the intensity of the battle between God's kingdom and the kingdom of the Evil One. Certainly Jesus' power over the "legion of demons" encouraged God's people by indicating that the Roman Empire one day would be replaced by the kingdom of heaven. It would not happen through violence but by the power of Jesus, whose life, taken by the legions of Rome, was the sacrifice by which the evil empires and kingdoms of this world are destroyed.

2. The challenge the demon-possessed man shouted (Mark 5:7) was literally, "Why are you interfering with us?" In plain English, the demons commanded, "Mind your own business."

   a. When had Jesus heard this challenge before, and what was the result? (See Mark 1:23 – 26.)

   b. The Evil One clearly does not want his kingdom, his reign, his subjects to be disturbed. So we can expect opposition and conflict as we represent God's kingdom in our world. What does Jesus' success in defeating the power of Satan's demons reveal about who really "owns" this world?

c. What assurance do we have that when we do God's
    will and seek to extend his kingdom and reclaim what
    is rightfully his that we will succeed in plundering the
    enemy? (See 1 Peter 5:8 – 11; James 4:7.)

3. What weapons has God given to every Jesus-follower that
    will enable us to resist and overcome the power of the Evil
    One? (See Ephesians 6:10 – 17.)

How different are these weapons from the weapons of the
kingdom of this world (Satan's) kingdom?

How well do these weapons suit warriors who are to accurately display God's kingdom in all that they say and do?

DID YOU KNOW?

Demonology and exorcism were very common in antiquity. Jews and Gentiles alike feared the gods, good and evil spirits, and demonic forces. The Gentiles tried to manipulate these forces with sacrifices, charms, offerings, spells, and sacred formulas. But Jesus came casting out demons through God's redeeming power. Whether or not others understood what was happening, Satan surely knew that the kingdom of God had arrived! His kingdom would not be able to stand against the power of a life wholly submitted — heart, soul, mind, and strength — to God.

4. When the man from the tombs was restored to his right mind, what was he eager to do? (See Mark 5:18.)

Instead of allowing his request, Jesus sent the man home to tell his own community what God had done for him! We may think of him as an unlikely ambassador for God's kingdom, but what did he accomplish? (See Mark 5:19 – 20.)

Anyone who had known or heard of the demoniac before he encountered Jesus knew instantly that something beyond their capacity to accomplish had happened to this man. His life proved his own story. In what ways did his life before

Jesus illustrate the reality of the Evil One's kingdom of death? In what ways did his life after Jesus represent the life-giving kingdom of God? (See Mark 5:3 – 5, 14 – 16, 19 – 20.)

5. When God's kingdom comes, it cannot be contained! Although Jesus rarely went into Gentile regions that were in the grip of the Evil One, those who were in bondage in those lands heard of the goodness of God's kingdom and sought out Jesus. (See Matthew 4:23 – 25.)

    a. Jesus ministered throughout Galilee. From how far away did people come to experience the blessing of his kingdom? (Refer to the map of Galilee and the Decapolis on page 24.)

    b. What do you think attracted them to Jesus, and what role do you think offering practical assistance to people facing the difficulties of life plays in displaying the true nature of God and his kingdom?

Reflection

When Jesus defeated the kingdom of the Evil One by driving away demons and setting their human hosts free, he validated his proclamation in Matthew 10:7 that the "kingdom of heaven has come near." That is true for his disciples as well. We are God's partners in the extension of his kingdom. We have been commissioned to bear witness through our words and lives that the King has come, the kingdom is coming, and the strong man has been bound so the Lord will plunder his house and restore to himself those who have been in bondage to evil.

Certainly we will face challenges along the way. It is likely that the man from the tombs faced some skeptics, people who didn't want him around, or people who feared the power of his message. But the reign of God in his heart and the power of what God had done for him could not be denied, and it defeated the power of the Evil One again and again. When Paul faced "storms" of interference from the kingdom of the Evil One on his way to Rome, God told him to keep up his courage, ride out the storm, and proclaim that Jesus is Lord. God's message to all of us who join in the great struggle between good and evil is still "press on" and "keep up your courage" as we face opposition from the Evil One.

> Do you think there was a way for Jesus to bring God's kingdom without confronting the kingdom of this world? Is there a way for us? Explain your answer.

> What opposition do you, as a disciple of Jesus today, face when you confront the strong man's kingdom in your world?

To what extent do you prepare yourself to use the weapons God has provided to wage war against the kingdom of the Evil One?

What joy do you experience when you see God's kingdom break out into territory that the Evil One has claimed for himself?

Memorize

For though we live in the world, we do not wage war as the world does. The weapons we fight with are not the weapons of the world. On the contrary, they have divine power to demolish strongholds.

2 Corinthians 10:3 – 4

Study 3 | Hellenism Then — and Now

The Very Words of God

As for you, you were dead in your transgressions and sins, in which you used to live when you followed the ways of this world and of the ruler of the kingdom of the air, the spirit who is now at work in those who are disobedient. All of us also lived among them at one time, gratifying the cravings of our flesh and following its desires and thoughts. Like the rest, we were by nature deserving of wrath. But because of his great love for us, God, who is rich in mercy, made us alive with Christ ...

Ephesians 2:1 – 5

Bible Discovery

Which Kingdom Reigns in Our Lives?

From the beginning, the kingdom of this world, which is based on the nature of the Evil One, has preached the gospel of the god named "me."[13] Satan's original temptation and the sin of our ancestors centered on one issue: doing what seemed right and good for them and elevating themselves as gods above their Creator. That also was the predominant view of Hellenism and the Roman Empire that ruled the world in which God's people lived during the first century.

The kingdom of heaven that Jesus came to bring is diametrically opposed to the kingdom of the Evil One who seduces God's children to reject the ways of their Creator. The kingdom of heaven brings life — abundant life[14] — to all who walk in the ways of Jesus, to all who faithfully obey and serve God. But everyone the Evil One entices to travel his paths will be destroyed as surely and as completely as the man from the tombs.

The glory that was Rome promoted a Hellenistic lifestyle that assigned value to people based on achieving enough wealth, renown, or power to have leisure time to enjoy whatever pleasures might be desired. The more one had, the more one could have and the more one could demand being served by others. That was the mad pursuit of the world's kingdom in which the Jews of Jesus' day found themselves. No wonder Jesus taught his disciples that they were not to be like the Gentiles! The citizens of that world did not represent the nature of those who serve the kingdom of heaven.

1. When Jesus cast the demons out of the man from the tombs, people noticed. Just try to imagine the scene of thousands of pigs stampeding into the Sea of Galilee where they drowned! Read the account in Mark 5:11 – 17 and answer the following questions.

   a. Do you think people from the nearby city who came to see what had happened were more interested in the change in the man who had been possessed by demons or more concerned about what happened to all of those

income-producing pigs? Explain your answer, including
which kingdom each option represents.

b. Although the people had witnessed the transforming
    power of the kingdom of heaven in the man from the
    tombs, why do you think they did not want Jesus to
    remain with them, and what about the kingdom of
    heaven is threatening to people who are bound to the
    kingdom of this world?

c. What insight into the Hellenistic values behind their
    response and the consequences of loving the kingdom of
    this world do you gain from Matthew 16:26 and 1 John
    2:15 – 17?

2. Before God led the Israelites into the Promised Land, he
    warned them about the dangers of the prosperity they would
    enjoy. What is the risk of comfort and plenty, and what
    impact can such a life have on our ability to extend God's
    kingdom in the world? (See Deuteronomy 6:10 – 12.)

3. The Evil One reigns over the kingdom of this world, offering all kinds of pleasure and self-serving enticements to get people to ignore and forget about God. Where does the path of those who bind themselves to the Evil One lead, and what is life like in his kingdom? (See Romans 1:21 – 25, 28 – 31; 1 Peter 4:3 – 4.)

DATA FILE
Hippos: Grand Prosperity on the Sea of Galilee
The Decapolis city of Hippos, or Susita as it was known to the Jews, towered atop a steep hill 1,200 feet above the eastern shore of the Sea of Galilee. In full view from Capernaum, the farmers and fishermen of Galilee could see evidence of the powerful, sophisticated, and modern world of the Decapolis barely eight miles away. It must have seemed both menacing and alluring to followers of the Torah who lived in the family- and community-oriented small towns of Galilee. *(cont.)*

THE FORUM OF HIPPOS HAD A BEAUTIFUL VIEW OF THE SEA OF GALILEE.

Alexander the Great's desire to "Hellenize" or make Greek the entire world was alive and well in Hippos. The city was thoroughly influenced by Greek culture in religion, political structure, and values. The Roman-style city was beautiful and prosperous. A large public forum, a theater, and beautifully carved columns, bases, and podia of limestone, granite, and white marble have been excavated there.

The city's prosperity was in part due to the fertile farmland it controlled to the east, which produced significant quantities of grain that were in high demand to feed the city of Rome. Harvested grain was transported down the Roman road to the Sea of Galilee, sailed across the sea, taken overland to the harbor at Caesarea, and then loaded on ships bound for Rome. The hilltop city of Hippos was somewhat limited in size due to its lack of readily accessible water, but a carved basalt pipeline transported the city's water supply from ten miles away.

A MARBLE CAPITAL EXCAVATED AT HIPPOS HINTS AT THE BEAUTY AND PROSPERITY OF THE CITY.

4. Jesus knew how subtle and cunning the Evil One is in drawing God's human creation away from the Creator and his kingdom. So his teaching frequently highlights the contrast between the priorities of God's kingdom and the priorities of the kingdom of this world. He repeatedly warns those of us who follow him of the dangers of committing ourselves to seek material things we want (and soon think we need) and perpetuating a lifestyle of acquisition and consumption.

As you read the following passages, take note of the differences in the priorities of the kingdom of heaven and the kingdom of the Evil One — what God values compared to the self-serving pursuits of money, fame, pleasure, and power.

Think about how these priorities would have been evident in Jesus' world and how they are evident in your world. Consider how each of these priorities advances one kingdom as opposed to the other.

The Text	Priorities of the Kingdom of God	Priorities of the Kingdom of This World
Matthew 5:43–45		
Matthew 6:25–33		
Luke 6:27–36		
Galatians 5:19–25		

5. We cannot be God's message and extend the reign of his kingdom if the other kingdom rules in our hearts. What can keep the knowledge of the Word of God and our desire to serve God's kingdom from taking root and being effective in our lives? (See Matthew 6:19–21, 24; 13:22.)

DATA FILE
Satan's Kingdom in First-Century Jewish Lands

To the first-century Jewish people, idolatry was the root of evil because wherever the Lord's kingship is not recognized and another deity is honored, every kind of immorality and depravity reigns. Idolatry is not simply a religious issue. If God's kingship over all things is not recognized, there are social, political, and economic implications because idolatry, oppression of the weak, and bloodshed (especially of the innocent) all go together. As the sages explained it, the evil and immorality of the Gentile world was rooted in their rampant idolatry. *(cont.)*

The Jewish people were subject to Rome, an empire devoted to the worship of many gods, not the least of which was the emperor himself. The Romans built temples for their gods everywhere. They erected statues and dedication plaques for divine Caesar in public places, claiming the territory as Caesar's own. Some scholars believe there were between 25,000 and 50,000 statues and plaques of Caesar Augustus alone throughout the Roman Empire![15] Local authorities invited people to worship Caesar in every province they controlled. They often mocked, and later brutally persecuted, those who refused. Caesar's portrait was often stamped on coins, depicting him as a divine being.

To the Jews, who were devoted to worshiping God alone, the idolatrous statues and depictions on coins defiled their land and were an affront to their God. They were ever-present reminders that, for the time being, idolatry had the upper hand. Adding to the wickedness of the Romans and other Gentiles, they did not acknowledge the Lord as King and did not obey his commands. Not only did they live in ways God had forbidden, they failed to conduct themselves for the good of others. "Love your neighbor or even your enemy" was not carved on Roman plaques. There was no compassion for those in need, for the poor, for the alien, or for the widow and orphan.

Reflection

Today most of us live in areas not unlike the Hellenistic cities of the Decapolis where the humanistic priorities of the kingdom of this world reign. We appreciate some of the comforts and benefits of that kingdom — and all too easily chase after its self-serving values. Those of us who claim to follow Jesus face temptations in virtually all areas of life to go our own way, choose our own path, and make our own choices regarding which of God's commands we will obey. But we cannot serve two kingdoms. We must decide which kingdom we will serve and then guard against sabotaging our own story.

The account of Jesus going to the other side and setting free the man from the tombs who had been held captive by the Evil One has a profound lesson for God's people who live in prosperous cultures today.

Jesus demonstrated to his disciples, and Bible readers ever since, that to expand God's kingdom and extend his reign involves practical action. The proof that the kingdom of heaven is present in the community of God's people is the evidence that good overcomes evil.

It is difficult for a humanist to find value in those who have little to contribute to society. In a culture that marks one's worth by what is accomplished or accumulated, or by power or beauty, people such as the unborn, the homeless, the poor, the disabled, the alien, the mentally ill, and the old have little value. It is easy to push them and their needs aside, demanding that they pull themselves up by their bootstraps or believe it and achieve it and make something of themselves.

In contrast, when God's people bring about justice for the oppressed, provide for the poor, support the weak and infirm, and invite the lonely into caring community, the Evil One's chaos is driven away and the kingdom of God breaks forth. When businesses are run with honesty and integrity, employees are paid fair wages, workers do their very best in their jobs, racism is rejected, and gossip is never practiced, Satan's power is defeated and God's kingdom comes.

It seems to me that one of the great failures of followers of Jesus today is that we accept a level of unrighteousness that *invalidates* God's kingdom. If we do not overcome evil with good, we fail to prove the validity of God's kingdom. This hits home, doesn't it? I know it hits home to me. It's challenging to resist the pull of Satan's kingdom, to remain focused on God and to be his spiritual light shining into spiritually dark places.

We must ask ourselves, at what point has our wealth and prosperity become so important to us that we are unwilling to use it to bring God's *shalom* to those who are oppressed by chaos? Do we really want Jesus to stop challenging the community of faith today and leave us alone in our comfortable world? Are we really content to accept racist attitudes, pursue wealth, slander our opponents, and display apathy toward those in need and in so doing lose our opportunities to demonstrate that God's kingdom is among us?

The big question for each of us is, does your life deny or validate your story?

To what extent are you valuing the "pigs" more highly than people who are hurting?

To what extent have you been unwilling to live a life that extends God's kingdom into a desperate world because you are still holding on to dimensions of your former life that gratify "the cravings of our flesh ... its desires and thoughts" (Ephesians 2:3)?

If you still spend time in the "tombs" you used to live in, you will never display God as he is; you will not advance his reign.

Memorize

Blessed is the one who does not walk in step with the wicked or stand in the way that sinners take or sit in the company of mockers, but whose delight is in the law of the LORD and who meditates on his law day and night.

Psalm 1:1–2

CRUCIFIXION: THE CORONATION OF A KING

Inspired by the Spirit of God, Mark began his account of the life and teaching of Jesus of Nazareth by proclaiming the good news — the gospel that Jesus was and is the Messiah, the Son of God. Mark kept emphasizing this truth throughout his book,[1] and even reported a Roman centurion at the foot of the cross stating that Jesus was the Son of God. His clear declaration of the person of Jesus has shaped the theology of the church and its profession that Jesus was both God and man, the promised ruler of all creation.

Many Christian scholars believe Mark's gospel is one of the earliest New Testament books,[2] likely written to Jesus-followers in Rome just before the Romans destroyed the Jewish nation and the temple in Jerusalem. If so, the claims he makes for Jesus no doubt were provocative and dangerous. Even if he did not write to the community of Jesus in Rome, his account proclaims Jesus to be Lord and God of all, which all but invalidates the emperor's claims. It also makes clear that *pax romana*, the Roman peace, is not the *shalom* promised by God in the Hebrew Bible.

In turbulent first-century Rome, there was more to Mark's choice of language about Jesus than we might realize. The terms *gospel*, *Messiah*, and *Son (of God)* define the person of Jesus and also parallel (and therefore, undermine) Roman beliefs and practices regarding the emperor's sovereignty and deity. Christians today usually assume that *gospel* is a religious word coined to describe news about Jesus, but *gospel* had deep cultural meaning for Jews and anyone under the rule of Imperial Rome. Announcements concerning the emperor — the birth of an imperial heir, a victory over Rome's enemies, the coronation of a new emperor, or in some cases simply an imperial announcement—were officially described as *good news* or *gospel.*

Mark's choice of the word *Messiah* (Hebrew, *mashiach* meaning "anointed") also conveyed a pointed message. The word technically referred to people who God anointed for a specific task—prophets, priests, and kings in particular. It was specifically applied to the coming King—the Messiah—and became a synonym for him. At the time Jesus was born, religious Jews commonly believed that the Messiah would appear as Lord of all to judge and punish the wicked and to establish God's *shalom* for his chosen people.

But Caesar, and in Jesus' time, Caesar Augustus, also claimed to be "Lord and God" of all and "Savior" of the world. So Mark's declaration of Jesus being God's anointed King and Lord of all clearly established that Jesus was everything the emperor claimed to be and more. Hence, Caesar was not who he claimed to be.

Mark's opening words introducing Jesus as the "Son of God" no doubt shocked Jews and Gentile Romans alike and fostered intense reactions far beyond what his words communicated about Caesar. After all, Pontius Pilate—Caesar's representative—had crucified Jesus and declared him to be an enemy of the state. How, then, could one claim that Jesus (and not Caesar) is Savior and Lord?

One might expect that a Jesus-follower would downplay the story of Jesus' crucifixion or ignore it altogether and concentrate on Jesus' successes in attracting crowds and performing miracles. Mark, however, did the opposite. He highlighted Jesus' great accomplishments as Messiah and made Jesus' suffering and agonizing execution a central part of his message. In fact, the cross is the very basis of Jesus' lordship over all. Mark's gospel—as one scholar brilliantly explains—is an apology, a defense of the cross.[3]

Mark's entire gospel focuses on Jesus' suffering and presents it as God's victory over sin, the Evil One, and death. His portrayal of the crucifixion appears to make that triumphant point subtly and powerfully.[4] Although emperors declared their lordship and deity in many ways, none was more dramatic or intentional than the Imperial Triumph. Mark, however, viewed Jesus' walk to the cross as an even greater Triumph. Would an audience that had recently experienced the Triumph of Nero have recognized the greater Triumph in the story of Jesus' walk to the cross? Let's see.

Opening Thoughts (3 minutes)

The Very Words of God

> *And being found in appearance as a man, he [Jesus] humbled himself by becoming obedient to death — even death on a cross! Therefore God exalted him to the highest place and gave him the name that is above every name, that at the name of Jesus every knee should bow, in heaven and on earth and under the earth, and every tongue acknowledge that Jesus Christ is Lord, to the glory of God the Father.*
>
> Philippians 2:8–11

Think About It

God often acts in ways quite opposite from what we might expect. To be great in God's kingdom, for example, is to be humble and to serve others. By generously sharing our treasure on earth, we gain treasure in heaven. Even the birth of Jesus — the King of kings and Lord of lords — seems far too modest to us. Why would the eternal King of heaven be born in a crude shelter for animals instead of a grand palace?

What challenges do such descriptions of the ways of God and his Son, Jesus, present for us when we share the gospel in a world that views bigger as better, wealth as power, and celebrity as worth?

How do you explain (or avoid explaining) God's flagrantly counter-cultural perspectives to people in your world?

Video Notes (29 minutes)

The message of Rome's glory

Caesar: a player in the gospel story

The Roman Triumph, a display of sovereignty and deity

Mark's presentation of the crucifixion of Jesus as a Triumph

The way of the cross, the path to glory

Video Discussion (9 minutes)

1. What in this presentation of a Roman Triumph as a metaphor for Jesus' sacrifice for all of humanity stood out to you, and why?

2. The Imperial Triumph made a powerful statement about the emperor and his reign to the people of the Roman Empire. To what extent do you imagine the display of power, drama, and glory would draw the hearts of the people into the kingdom of Rome's world — the kingdom of the Evil One?

3. Imagine what it was like for the early followers of Jesus, who likely were facing persecution from the Roman regime, to see Jesus' crucifixion as a Triumph! How do you think it may have affected their faithfulness to obey him in all things and walk in his ways?

How does what you have learned about a Triumph change your picture of what Jesus accomplished on the way to the cross?

What impact does Jesus' Triumph have on you, and how does it influence your understanding of what it means (and what it may require) to follow Jesus?

4. As modern Westerners, we marvel at the Colosseum as a grand ancient structure, not realizing the statement it made about the kingdom of God and the kingdom of this world: because it was built in part with the plunder of Jerusalem and the temple, the gods of Rome are greater than the God of the Jews.

    How hard do you think it was for believers in Rome to explain the greatness and worthiness of a seemingly "lesser" God to people in their world?

    In what ways does our culture perceive God to be "lesser" — the God who judges, the God who doesn't do enough to alleviate human suffering, the God who requires obedience, etc. — and in what ways is it difficult to display him as he is to people in our world?

5. On the map of the ancient city of Rome, follow the path of a Roman Triumph. It began at the Praetorium, followed the *Via Sacra* through the city, through the forum of Augustus and Caesar, passed Mars Ultor, and then up to Capitoline Hill and the temple of Jupiter.

FIRST-CENTURY ROME

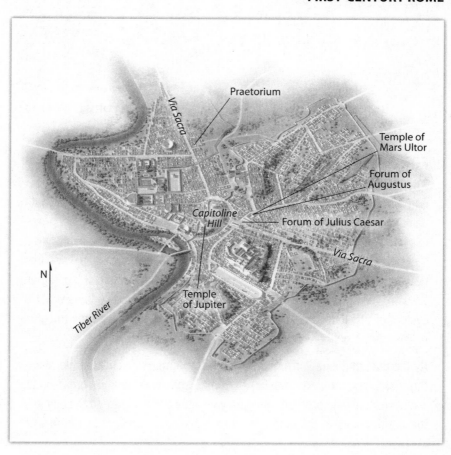

On the map of the ancient city of Jerusalem, follow the steps of Jesus to the cross. He began at the Praetorium (Herod's Palace), then trod the *Via Dolorosa* to Golgotha, which is now the Church of the Holy Sepulchre.[5]

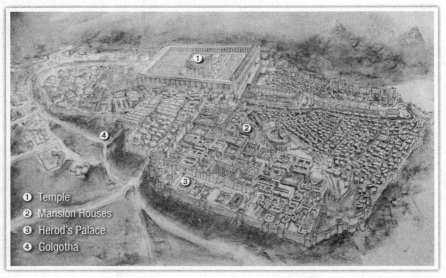

- ❶ Temple
- ❷ Mansion Houses
- ❸ Herod's Palace
- ❹ Golgotha

FIRST-CENTURY JERUSALEM

FOR GREATER UNDERSTANDING
Imperial Rome: The Cost of Greatness

Rome began as a small farming village on the Tiber River[6] during the eighth century BC. Its inhabitants, the Etruscans, were known for their military prowess and transformed their village into a walled city. By the first century BC, they had built an empire that spread throughout the Mediterranean, north into Gaul, and east into Asia Minor and Syria (see page 63 for a map of the Roman Empire). The Etruscans also established Rome's pantheon of gods, its political system of provinces that answered to the Roman Senate, and the imperial policies that brought a constant flow of resources into the city.

By the time of Jesus' birth, Rome was the commercial center of the Mediterranean, and the upper classes of Roman society were quite prosperous. A massive building program funded by wealthy Romans turned the city into the greatest city in the world. But to support such prosperity, Rome was forced to expand its territory and demand for raw materials and slaves from its provinces.

The power to expand and control its empire required increasing numbers of legions drawn initially from the Roman population. Many legionaries were absent from their farms for extended periods of time and sold them to wealthy landowners in order to support their families. When their duty was finished, many of them returned to Rome seeking work. In addition, people from Italy, Greece, and eventually the far reaches of the empire came to Rome seeking a better life. But, as many contemporary societies are learning, there was not enough demand for labor to meet the needs of all the immigrants.

An extensive social welfare system was developed to provide for the poor, and by 25 BC, Caesar Augustus had established a daily ration of grain for the growing underclass. The constant need to provide for the majority of Rome's population in order to maintain peace and calm made the distant provinces of the empire ever more important in providing food and resources. Meanwhile, the slave population continued to grow. Some scholars believe that as many as half of Rome's inhabitants were slaves, comprising the majority of almost every occupation—domestic servants for the wealthy, construction workers, craftsmen, artisans, prostitutes, and even lower-level public servants. Rome's prosperity became completely dependent on the slave class.

Rome changed from being a republic governed by the Senate to an imperial kingdom led by an emperor, in part due to the growing difficulties involved in preserving the prosperity of the wealthy and sustaining social order among the lower classes. Emperors were able to sustain their lofty position only as long as they appeased lower economic classes. The need to increase the empire's wealth and establish the emperor's right to reign contributed to the increased importance of the emperor's deification and his divine right to rule. In that process, the Triumph played a significant role.

Small Group Bible Discovery and Discussion (15 minutes)

Understanding the Path to the Cross in Light of a Roman Triumph

The Roman Triumph was a procession in which victorious generals, and later no one but the reigning emperor, marched through Rome to present the spoils of conquest to the people of the city. The Triumph was a dramatic and powerful declaration of the emperor's sovereignty and deity, and it helped to build awe and excitement for his greatness among the people. Accounts by ancient historians have provided a clear and detailed picture of a Roman Triumph,[7] which adds great meaning to our understanding of Jesus' crucifixion as recorded in Mark's gospel.

According to tradition, Mark's gospel was written between 65 and 69 AD to followers of Jesus in Rome[8] who would have seen Emperor Nero's Triumph and coronation. Even though Mark did not use the word *Triumph* in describing Jesus' mission,[9] his audience would have noticed the similarities between Jesus' procession to the cross and the familiar practice of Imperial Triumph. Mark's gospel is an example of how Jesus' first followers defended the story of the cross and saw in it God's declaration that Jesus is both Lord and God. Although the purpose of Jesus' procession was similar to that of an emperor who had defeated his enemies — to declare his absolute authority and his triumph over sin and death and the Evil One — the nature of Jesus' procession was quite different. Let's consider Mark's account of the path Jesus took to the cross in light of the practices of a Roman Triumph.

1. A Triumph began at a military outpost outside Rome with the presence and support of the Praetorian Guard, an elite group of Roman citizen soldiers established by Caesar Augustus that became the emperor's personal unit. The Praetorian Guard was the most well-trained unit in the Roman army, and its presence and protection kept the emperor in power. After Jesus was tried by Pilate, where was he taken and who was there? (See Mark 15:16.)

2. The triumphator was given the purple robe from Jupiter's statue, and a laurel wreath, sometimes made of gold, was placed on his head. In mockery, what did Praetorian soldiers give Jesus and place on his head? (See Mark 15:17.)

3. The procession for a Roman Triumph began as Roman soldiers acclaimed Caesar as Lord and God. How did the soldiers "acclaim" Jesus? (See Mark 15:18–19.)

DID YOU KNOW?

The procession that accompanied the triumphator's chariot gave spectators an idea of the victory won. Not only were the spoils of war carried along — weapons, gold, silver, and jewelry — but also images of battle scenes and towns conquered. The procession marched to a flourish of trumpets, the beat of drums, and the aroma of incense — perhaps worth millions of dollars. The chained prisoners, the most prominent of whom were usually killed in the dungeon before the sacrifice was made to Jupiter, accompanied the triumphator's chariot. The triumphator was preceded by the lictors in red war dress. The magistrates and the senators also walked ahead of the chariot with the triumphator and his young children. Older boys accompanied the triumphator on horseback, as did his officers. The chariot was followed by Romans who had been liberated from slavery.

4. Monuments depicting Roman Triumphs often show a sacrificial bull, decorated with a garland around its neck being led in the procession along the *Via Sacra*. Next to the bull an official carries the ax to be used to kill the sacrificial animal. How did the way Jesus traveled along the *Via Dolorosa* (the way of grief, suffering, and pain) reflect his imminent sacrifice and the instrument of his execution?[10] (See Mark 15:20 – 21.)

5. Jesus' procession through Jerusalem that ended at Golgotha is not the Triumph of a king that we might anticipate, but was it what Jesus had expected? And what does it reveal about the power of his kingdom? (See Matthew 20:18 – 19; Mark 10:33 – 34; John 1:29, 35 – 37.)

DATA FILE
Golgotha: The Place of the Skull
Romans typically established set places for executions, especially crucifixions when bodies were often left hanging as examples of Rome's policy toward those who refused to submit to Imperial authority. Apparently that place in Jerusalem was Golgotha, which Mark translates from the Hebrew as "the place of the skull" (Mark 15:22). The Hebrew word used generally refers to a human head detached from the body. The implication is that Jesus was crucified at "head" hill or "the place of the head," which is a strong parallel to Capitoline Hill, the final destination of each Imperial Triumph.

6. After making its way past Mars Ultor, the procession continued up to Capitoline Hill and the temple of Jupiter. Capitoline, or "head" hill, was so named because of the myth that when the temple's foundation was laid, an intact human head was found in the earth.[11] Where did the soldiers lead Jesus to be crucified, and how would that have strengthened the metaphor between an Imperial Triumph and Jesus' crucifixion? (See Mark 15:22.)

DID YOU KNOW?

During a Triumph, wine was presented to the triumphator as the procession arrived at its destination, just before the sacrifice was made. In like fashion, wine mixed with myrrh was offered to Jesus when he reached Golgotha. Wine mixed with myrrh was an expensive delicacy in the Roman world, and there is no known custom of Romans providing it to condemned prisoners — especially those facing the humiliation of crucifixion. So Mark's account of this spiced drink of the rich being offered to Jesus emphasizes the mocking of Jesus as "King of the Jews" by the soldiers. This unusual detail adds a noteworthy connection between Jesus' procession and the Roman Triumph.

Later, while on the cross, Jesus was offered "sour wine" (Mark 15:36; Matthew 27:48) that he tasted and refused. Sour wine or "wine vinegar" (NIV) apparently was used to deaden pain or to make the crucified person sleepy. Jesus apparently was determined to be fully aware as he offered himself as the sacrificial lamb for sinners. The offer of this wine is probably an allusion to Psalm 69:21.

7. At the temple of Jupiter, just before the bull was sacrificed, the triumphator was offered a cup of wine that he rejected and poured out on the ground. What was Jesus offered when he arrived at the site of his sacrifice (Mark 15:23), and what did he do with it?

8. It was common to see the emperor flanked by two officials as he made a public appearance.[12] Who did the soldiers crucify at Jesus' left and right as he hung on the cross, and what kind of a statement may the soldiers have been making? (See Mark 15:27 – 32.)

9. Roman Triumphs were given to those who had killed the most, subjugated the most, destroyed the most, and had won great victories at the expense of those who lost. How did Jesus, who died for all, freeing all, restoring any who believed, and came completely at his own expense, achieve victory? (See Philippians 2:8 – 11.)

Faith Lesson (3 minutes)

Mark wrote to people in the Roman Empire who were familiar with Roman power and the shamefulness of crucifixion as the penalty for those who rejected the ways of Rome. For many people of Jesus' day (and people today as well) the idea of a crucified Lord was foolishness. But the cross is actually the story of God's great power — the power of servanthood and sacrifice as well as the exaltation of Jesus who gave himself for all humanity. Mark's message is clear: Jesus' walk to the cross and his brutal death by crucifixion[13] is actually his Triumph. The cross is not a defeat; it is a great victory!

Isaiah 53:1 – 12 prophesied that God intended Jesus' suffering to be used for our redemption. We are the condemned prisoners of Jesus' Triumph, but instead of being killed, Jesus gave his life as the sacrifice for the forgiveness of our sin. Through this act of humiliation and weakness, even to the point of death, God gave Jesus a place among the great.[14] God turned upside-down this world's view of power and victory. Through Jesus' crucifixion and resurrection, God overcame the power of sin, the Evil One, and the hold that sin and death had on all humanity. The greatest victory and power were not the result of violence and killing but of selfless sacrifice and dying![15]

Jesus expressed his strength, power, and lordship through the Triumph of his weakness, service, and sacrifice — not the Roman Triumph of war, victory, acclaim, and domination. Since true disciples imitate their rabbi, those of us who claim to be Jesus' disciples must also take up our crosses. To follow in the footsteps of Jesus and demonstrate to our broken world the true nature of God and his kingdom, we each are called to the life of servanthood and sacrifice that Jesus demonstrated for us.

This path at times can seem overwhelmingly painful. Even Jesus, as he hung on the cross, cried out to God in anguish, "My God, my God, why have you forsaken me?" (Mark 15:34). His cry was not simply an expression of separation from God's presence; it was a recitation of Psalm 22:1, a psalm that speaks of mockery and the agony of rejection even by God's people.

1.   As you read the following portions of Psalm 22, prayerfully consider what Jesus suffered — the cross he took up — on your behalf. Consider also the price — and the victory — of taking up your cross as you seek to advance God's kingdom in your world.

     • *Psalm 22:1*: My God, my God, why have you forsaken me? Why are you so far from saving me, so far from my cries of anguish?

     • *Psalm 22:6 - 8*: But I am a worm and not a man, scorned by everyone, despised by the people. All who see me mock me; they hurl insults, shaking their heads. "He trusts in the Lord," they say, "let the Lord rescue him. Let him deliver him, since he delights in him."

     • *Psalm 22:19, 24*: But you, Lord, do not be far from me. You are my strength; come quickly to help me ... For he has not despised or scorned the suffering of the afflicted one; he has not hidden his face from him but has listened to his cry for help.

     To what extent are you convinced that God is near, that he will hear you, and that he will answer your cries and lead you into the battle to extend his kingdom in your world?

Closing (1 minute)

Read 2 Corinthians 2:14 aloud together: "But thanks be to God, who always leads us as captives in Christ's triumphal procession and uses us to spread the aroma of the knowledge of him everywhere."

Then pray, thanking the Lord that Jesus was willing to walk the road to the cross. Praise him for being the King of kings whose power and unfailing love encompasses the grace to humble himself and face the scorn, mockery, jeering crowds, and a brutal death to save his people and bring forth his kingdom. Pray for the grace and commitment to learn how to walk as Jesus walked — in servanthood, humility, and sacrifice. May we be mindful of our brothers and sisters who are, even now, faithfully walking the path of persecution so that the influence of God's kingdom will grow. In the name of Jesus, our Savior, Amen.

Memorize

> *But thanks be to God, who always leads us as captives in Christ's triumphal procession and uses us to spread the aroma of the knowledge of him everywhere.*
>
> *2 Corinthians 2:14*

The Kingdom of Heaven Advances: Reclaiming What Belongs to God

In-Depth Personal Study Sessions

Study 1 | God's Kingdom Comes!

The Very Words of God

> *Let this Messiah, this king of Israel, come down now from the cross, that we may see and believe.*
>
> **Mark 15:32**

Bible Discovery

A Kingdom from Another Place

A person who received Imperial Roman justice by crucifixion would wear or carry a placard called a *titulus* that identified the crime. Someone likely carried that placard during Jesus' procession to the cross on the *Via Dolorosa*. When he was crucified, the inscription was placed above him on the cross. The charge for which Imperial Rome crucified him was simply "King of the Jews."[16]

Those who placed the *titulus* above Jesus had no idea how accurate the charge was. By accepting and declaring the title "Messiah," Jesus identified himself as Israel's King — the Anointed One. By proclaiming that the kingdom of heaven had arrived when he came to earth, Jesus identified himself as the true King of that kingdom.

As Jesus emphasized to Pilate,[17] however, Jesus' kingdom was from another place, not from this world. Like Pilate, many people (even Jews), thought the Messiah's kingdom would be much like the kingdom of Rome, not like the kingdom from another world that Jesus came to bring. Let's consider how different these two kingdoms were.

1. Mark 15:25 – 32 shows the disdain many onlookers had for Jesus and who he claimed to be.

    a. As Jesus hung on the cross, what kinds of people insulted him?

    b. What was the nature of their insults, and what do you think they had expected Jesus to be or do for them?

POINT TO PONDER
Why Didn't Jesus Save Himself?

Naked, Jesus was nailed to the cross and elevated above a jeering crowd.[18] Even passersby apparently knew him and his teaching well enough to mock him for not saving himself from brutal execution. One wonders whether their derision echoes their desire for a conquering Messiah who would overthrow their Roman occupiers. Had they expected from Jesus the same dominating conquest of their enemies that Caesar and the nations around them practiced?

Of course Jesus could have saved himself. After all, he saved others from the penalty of their sins, from isolation from God, from the loneliness of being outcasts, from disease and hunger, and even from the social humiliation of running out of wine at a wedding! Jesus could have saved himself, but he represented a kingdom that wasn't from this world. So he chose to save others rather than himself.

Such sacrifice for the benefit of others wasn't the Roman way. Roman emperors could have sacrificed their own interests for the benefit of the

Empire and its people, but history shows most did the opposite. They used their power and influence to gain as much as they could for themselves and their inner circle. Their Triumphs brought wealth at the expense of those they had conquered and those who cheered and acclaimed them as they paraded on the *Via Sacra*.

Seeking to dominate others and wanting to be elevated to positions of honor is not the way of Jesus' kingdom. Jesus' way to glory and triumph is the way of humiliation and sacrifice. He gave his life for the benefit of others and took nothing for himself. Who in the kingdom of Rome could imagine such a thing? No wonder people mocked and scornfully acclaimed the idea of Jesus as a king. Paradoxically, their scornful acclamation of Jesus actually declared the truth! He was — and is — Messiah and King, the One who saves all humankind.

2. Caesar's Triumph celebrated his ability to force others to serve him, but Jesus' walk to the cross demonstrated his desire to serve others. In Caesar's kingdom, which was under the influence of the Evil One, greatness was measured by accomplishment, accumulation, beauty, and power. How is greatness measured in Jesus' kingdom? (See Matthew 18:1 – 5; 20:25 – 28.)

3. Whereas Caesar's kingdom came to those who exerted political and military power and dominated other people — often through brutal persecution — to whom does Jesus' kingdom come, and how is it demonstrated? (See Matthew 5:3 – 11.)

DATA FILE
The Imperial Forums — Monuments to Rome

The Imperial Forums of Rome (Latin, *Fora*, plural) consist of a series of monumental public squares constructed between 50 BC and 125 AD. These forums were the centers of politics, religion, and economics in the first-century world and in a sense reflect the beating heart of the Roman Empire. The most ancient, the Roman Forum, was the venue for public gatherings in Rome as well as for the government. In order to symbolize his absolute power, Julius Caesar constructed a large forum as an extension of the Roman Forum that predated it and gave it his name.

In 42 BC, Augustus and Mark Antony avenged Julius Caesar's assassination by defeating the legions of Brutus and Cassius at the battle of Philippi. In honor of this victory, Augustus vowed to build a temple to Mars Ultor ("Mars the Avenger"), whom he believed gave him the victory. In 2 BC, after forty years of construction, the Temple of Mars Ultor in the Forum of Augustus adjacent to the Forum of Julius Caesar was inaugurated. This forum complex has long, deep porticos with two large semicircular apses where public discussion ensued. State ceremonies and war planning took place there. Plunder from victories was displayed there for the official Triumphs that passed by on the *Via Sacra*.

TEMPLE OF MARS ULTOR

The design and decoration of the Forum of Augustus expressed the ideology of Augustus by depicting his absolute power and his claim to be the Son of God, the son of deified Julius. The Forum also proclaimed the Roman worldview that peace came by piety (worship of the gods), war, victory, and peace. Many statues of Augustus in full military uniform were displayed in the center of the Forum.

4. In contrast to Caesar's kingdom where raw power forced
    people to obey his commands, what are Jesus' followers to do
    willingly and teach others to do? (See Matthew 5:19; 7:21.)

5. In Caesar's kingdom, those in power took what they needed and
    showed concern for others only as it provided benefit for them-
    selves. In contrast, how important are our needs in the kingdom
    of God, and how are they met? (See Matthew 6:31 – 33.)

PERSONAL PROFILE
The First Emperor

This magnificent, first-century statue found in Aphrodias, Turkey, is believed to be of Caesar Augustus (September 23, 63 BC–August 19, 14 AD). He was born Gaius Octavius into a wealthy Roman family, then adopted by Julius Caesar and designated as his heir. Viewed as the founder of the Roman Empire, Caesar Augustus ruled as its first emperor from 27 BC until he died. Following his victory over Cassius and Brutus at Philippi to avenge his father's death, he ruled Rome with Mark Antony and Marcus Lepidus. Eventually he expelled Lepidus and defeated Antony at Actium in 31 BC. He then ruled as a dictator using the authority granted to him for life by the Senate.

STATUE OF CAESAR AUGUSTUS

Augustus instituted an era of peace called *Pax Romana* (Roman Peace), extended the empire significantly, developed a system of paved roads, created the Praetorian Guard, launched a massive building program, restored or built eighty-two temples, and spread the Roman cult worldwide. Most significant, he proclaimed his father's deification and declared himself "Son of God." During his reign, worship of Augustus as Lord and God spread throughout the empire as dictated by law, required ritual, payment of tribute, and by the titles on coins, statues such as the one shown on the facing page, and carvings.

Reflection

Although Caesar may have proclaimed Imperial Rome to be a divinely sovereign and eternal kingdom, it was merely a kingdom of this world. It was crumbling even as Mark's gospel was being written. No conquest of new lands, no acclamation of the crowds, no accumulation of wealth, and no cruel enforcement of its values could sustain it.

It is easy to be seduced by the kingdoms of this world and expect God's kingdom to exert itself in the same ways. During Jesus' Triumph to the cross, the mocking — but true — chants of acclamation came from minds that were closed to the nature of God and his redemptive kingdom. People expected, and preferred, Jesus' kingdom to be of this world. They expected dominating conquest and brutal execution of judgment. But this King had come riding a donkey, meek and humble. He came not to oppress but to suffer, not to kill but to die for the very people who hated him. And although Caesar's kingdom is ancient history, the kingdom of Jesus — the kingdom of heaven — continues today and will last through all eternity.

Although it's easy to criticize the crowd's blindness to Jesus' message concerning his kingdom, we might ask if we are all that different in what we expect of his kingdom today. To what extent do we expect the kingdom of heaven to break out through political influence, military "solutions," financial security for ourselves, or protection of our "rights" without regard for the rights or well-being of others?

In terms of the world you live in, in what practical ways do you see the kingdom of Jesus differing from the "kingdom of Caesar" or the "kingdom of this world"?

In what ways does Jesus, through his Triumph of sacrifice and suffering, help you to better understand the cost of taking up your cross and following him?

In what ways does his example demonstrate what it looks like to suffer for other people and sacrificially put others' interests ahead of your own?

Memorize

My kingdom is not of this world. If it were, my servants would fight to prevent my arrest by the Jewish leaders. But now my kingdom is from another place.

John 18:36

Study 2 | Jesus: The True Son of God

The Very Words of God

> *And when the centurion, who stood there in front of Jesus, saw how he died, he said, "Surely this man was the Son of God!"*

> **Mark 15:39**

Bible Discovery

Signs of Divine Identity

At various times, Roman emperors declared their divinity — "Son of God" and "Lord and Savior" of their people — in connection with their Imperial Triumph.[19] So when Jesus came to earth and claimed to be God in the flesh, it was not the first time this had been said. In fact, the Caesars first claimed their divine status following the death of Julius Caesar three decades before Jesus' birth.

In order to validate their claims of divinity, Roman emperors looked for a portent — a presumed sign of approval from the gods that validated their deity. During Julius Caesar's memorial games, for example, a comet bright enough to be visible in broad daylight appeared. The priesthood, the Roman Senate, and his adopted son, Octavian (Caesar Augustus), took that as a sign that Julius Caesar had been deified and had ascended to the gods. Therefore, Octavian claimed to be "Savior of the world" and "Son of God" at his coronation in 27 BC.

Given the claims of the Roman emperors at the time of Jesus, it is interesting to note that God provided signs that Jesus was his Son, the Son of God. At various times in Jesus' life, God showed his approval and vindication of his Son. Jesus' Triumph, ending in his death on the cross, was no exception. In fact, the supernatural occurrences that accompanied his death reveal God's presence and affirm that Jesus' crucifixion was part of God's plan for the redemption of humanity from sin.

1. From the very beginning of his life, Jesus was presented as the Son of God. Notice how Mark began his gospel: "The beginning of the gospel about Jesus Christ, the Son of God."[20]

    a. What unusual signs accompanied the birth of Jesus, and what impact did those signs have on the people who saw them? (See Luke 2:8 – 16; Matthew 2:1 – 2, 9 – 11.)

    b. What sign affirmed Jesus' identity as the Son of God immediately after he was baptized by John? (See Matthew 3:16 – 17; Mark 1:9 – 11.)

2. As recorded in Mark 15:33, what foreboding phenomenon occurred as Jesus was dying on the cross? How might people who witnessed what was happening — particularly the Jews and soldiers who arrested Jesus — have interpreted the meaning of these events, and what might they have wondered about Jesus as a result? (See Joel 2:1, 10 – 11, 31; Luke 22:52 – 53.)

    Who was certainly present and in complete control of what was happening as Jesus died? (See Genesis 1:2 – 5.)

3. Upon Jesus' death, which marked the completion of his blood sacrifice for the forgiveness of sin, what happened in God's temple in Jerusalem? (See Mark 15:37 – 38; Hebrews 10:19 – 22.)

    What did this mean for all people, and what did it reveal about Jesus and his true identity?

4. When Jesus died, what else happened outside the city of Jerusalem that was possible only through divine power, and what did it indicate about Jesus' deity and what he had accomplished on the cross? (See Matthew 27:50 – 52.)

5. What impact did all that he had seen of Jesus' Triumph and death on the cross have on the Roman centurion in charge of guarding Jesus? (See Matthew 27:54; Mark 15:39.)

In what ways did his declaration about Jesus conflict with his loyalty oath that proclaimed Caesar as Lord and God, and what does that say about the power of Jesus' triumph over the Evil One?

What does the centurion's declaration about Jesus say about the claim of Caesar Augustus, and his son Tiberius, to be "Savior" of the world?

POINT TO PONDER
The Centurion's Testimony

A centurion held a position of high honor in the Roman military, leading as many as a thousand men. Highly trained, centurions led from the front lines and through their acts of bravery and valor gained the reputation of being the best soldiers in the world. When this Roman marine—a colonel—heard Jesus' loud cry and saw how he died, he testified, "Surely this man was the Son of God!" His commander-in-chief, Tiberius Caesar, claimed this same title—*divi filius*, Son of God—as had his father, Caesar Augustus. In Jesus, the centurion recognized the true "Son of God," which implies that he knew Caesar was not!

The centurion's testimony can be understood in several ways. If we emphasize the words *man* and *Son*, we mean "Jesus is God in human form." If we emphasize the word *God*, the point is that Jesus was (is) divine or God in flesh. In the case of the Roman officer, it is likely that the stress is on the word *this* as in "*this* man." Then the emphasis is on Jesus being the Son; therefore,

Caesar is not. Whether or not the centurion fully understood the theological meaning of his own witness, he gave the final acclamation of Jesus' triumphant walk to the cross—the very claim that Caesar made throughout his Triumph: "I am Lord and the divine Son of God." Jesus' Triumph indeed declared his true lordship and deity.

Reflection

For a Roman centurion to testify that Jesus is the Son of God made the gospel — the good news — politically and religiously dangerous. Such testimony was anti-Roman. The person testifying to such a claim would be an enemy of the state!

Although no evidence exists that believers were persecuted immediately following Jesus' crucifixion, the time would come when many of them were required to deny their commitment to Jesus as Lord and God or face Roman justice. In response, many early Jesus-followers sacrificed their lives to affirm exactly what the Roman officer acclaimed: Jesus is the living Son of God. Despite the claims against him, his execution did not make him a terrorist and traitor. Rather, his execution was a Triumph that declared him victorious — the true Lord and Son of God.

Why is the proclamation that Jesus is God's Son as important today as it was when he walked on earth?

What would be your acclamation of who Jesus has shown himself to be to you?

In what way does your testimony of who Jesus is go against what is politically or socially "correct" in the eyes of people in your world?

How high a price are you willing to pay to stand firm in declaring and demonstrating to your world the true identity of Jesus?

Memorize

And a voice from heaven said, "This is my Son, whom I love; with him I am well pleased."

Matthew 3:17

Study 3 | Jesus' Followers Continue the Mission

The Very Words of God

For the message of the cross is foolishness to those who are perishing, but to us who are being saved it is the power of God.

1 Corinthians 1:18

Bible Discovery

Take Up the Cross: The Great Triumph of Jesus

Jesus is portrayed in the Text as the Messiah who attracted great crowds, taught with authority, brought healing to the diseased and infirm, and defeated demonic powers. Yet Mark's account also describes Jesus quite differently, focusing on how he was persecuted and how he was rejected, even by his closest followers. Religious leaders condemned him, crowds demanded his execution, and the political authority acquiesced by crucifying him. The One who came to bring salvation, eternal life, and true hope to all of humanity suffered a painful, shameful death — a penalty that was reserved for the worst criminals, enemies of the people, and terrorists.

In Mark's account, however, there is no contradiction between Jesus' popularity and accomplishments and his shame and suffering. Rather than being a defeat, Jesus' suffering and death on the cross is shown to be his greatest accomplishment! By taking up his cross and its shame, Jesus proved his divine sonship and demonstrated his power over the Evil One's kingdom of sin and death.

As King of kings and Lord of all, Jesus accepted the mission God had given to Israel — to be a priest to the nations, to mediate and demonstrate the very nature of God to a world that does not know him. Those of us who follow Jesus are now called to take up our cross and faithfully continue the mission God gave to Israel. We are to be living witnesses of the God we serve and to have the mind of Christ, who humbled himself to be the suffering servant so that all of humanity could be redeemed.

1. Jesus' crucifixion is a Triumph turned upside down. It is an eternal victory and not the shameful defeat it was intended to be. We who are Jesus' disciples do not need to be ashamed of his gospel no matter how strange or misunderstood it may seem to those who do not know him. Jesus is Lord and God, not Caesar. Who did Jesus conquer by his sacrificial death, and what would be the result of that accomplishment? (See John 12:31 – 33.)

2. Using the metaphors of a Triumph, 2 Corinthians 2:14 – 16
    describes those who follow Jesus as being "captives in Christ's
    triumphal procession" and the "pleasing aroma of Christ."

    a. In light of what you've learned about the Roman Tri-
        umph and how it compares to Jesus' Triumph, in what
        way are we "conquered" by his victory on the cross? Or,
        to put it another way, in what ways does the cross make
        us servants, and in what ways does it set us free? (See
        1 Corinthians 7:22.)

    b. Remembering the incense altars that were placed along
        the route of a Roman Triumph to remind the Romans
        that Caesar is "Lord" and "God," what is the purpose of
        being the "aroma" of Christ among our fellow believers
        and those who do not yet know him as Lord and Savior?

3. What does Matthew 16:24 – 26 reveal about what the cross
    motivates followers of Jesus to do?

4. What do we learn from Isaiah 53:1 – 6, 10 – 12 and John
    14:9 – 13 about the power of God's loving, sacrificial, suffer-
    ing nature toward all of humanity and how Jesus revealed it?

5. Jesus, the Son of God, willingly took up his cross and became a suffering servant in order to accomplish the mission of making God known. How does the apostle Paul say that followers of Jesus are to take up the cross and make God known? (See Philippians 2:2 – 11.)

6. In what ways does 1 Corinthians 1:18 – 25 encourage us to continue pursuing the mission God has given to us and have confidence in the message of Christ even though it may be misunderstood and rejected by those who do not know God?

DID YOU KNOW?

Paul mentioned Triumph twice to the communities of Jesus in Colossae and Corinth. To the Colossians, apparently using Imperial Triumphs as a metaphor for Jesus' crucifixion, Paul celebrated Jesus' victorious Triumph of the cross over the rulers and authorities of this world (Colossians 2:15). This certainly brought to mind the practice of including conquered prisoners — especially rulers — in Rome's Triumph processions. Whereas Jesus' experiences involved sacrifice and suffering, Imperial Triumphs focused on dominance and military victory.

In his letter to the Corinthians, Paul used Triumph more specifically to compare the Imperial Triumph's handling of prisoners and use of incense altars to the believers' role as members of Jesus' Triumph. He wrote, "But thanks be to God, who always leads us as captives in Christ's triumphal procession and uses us to spread the aroma of the knowledge of him everywhere" (2 Corinthians 2:14). Certainly the authors and their audiences were aware of a Triumph and could use it as a metaphor for their own faith walk.

Reflection

Jesus' suffering on the cross resulted in victory over Satan's kingdom and death. Through his sacrificial Triumph, we are released to experience true freedom. Jesus has given us freedom and life in one sense and the opportunity to become his servants or slaves in another sense. We can choose to serve others — or not. We can choose to be the aroma of Jesus — or not. But if we want to be true disciples of Jesus, if we want God's kingdom to come, we have a cross to take up just as Jesus our Savior took up his cross.

We don't like to hear that. Even Jesus' disciples wanted a kingdom without a cross. They expected God's kingdom to come as the Messiah crushed the power of Rome — not as he hung on a cross. They couldn't imagine that God's kingdom would come by love and sacrifice and suffering for one's enemies.

In our day, many of us seem to want a cross without a kingdom.[21] We tend to think that Jesus has done the dirty work of suffering so that we don't have to. We much prefer to enjoy the benefits of Jesus' cross and be blessed with prosperity without obediently taking up our cross, going to the other side, serving on behalf of others, and thereby extending God's reign in dark places.

Caesar's kingdom provided great benefit for the wealthy and powerful at the expense of most. Jesus' kingdom, on the other hand, came to benefit all, particularly the poor and marginalized, at his expense so that all people would come to know God. Recognizing the opposing values of these two kingdoms, and out of grateful obedience to God, the early communities of believers began to share everything they had with anyone who was needy rather than creating a society of patronage where a person only gives to others if there is benefit to be gained.

What will it require of you to take up your cross as Jesus did and do whatever is necessary to display the nature of God to a broken world? What sacrifices are you willing to make to obey the will of God so that his kingdom will reign and advance to take back territory the Evil One has stolen?

Paul challenges those who follow Jesus to recognize that God has selected us to be the aroma, the scent of Messiah, to everyone — permeating the world with God's presence — for the benefit of those who believe in Jesus and receive his salvation as well as those who do not and are perishing in sin.

Will you be faithful to take up that challenge?

Memorize

But thanks be to God, who always leads us as captives in Christ's triumphal procession and uses us to spread the aroma of the knowledge of him everywhere. For we are to God the pleasing aroma of Christ among those who are being saved and those who are perishing. To the one we are an aroma that brings death; to the other, an aroma that brings life. And who is equal to such a task?

2 Corinthians 2:14 – 16

ASCENSION: THE KING TAKES HIS THRONE

Most Christians today do not commemorate Jesus' ascension as part of our worship experience. We celebrate Jesus' birth, the arrival of Messiah, with cantatas and pageants complete with shepherds, wise men, and white-garbed angels (Herod, however, is noticeably ignored). We also gather on Good Friday and Resurrection Day to remember our Savior's suffering on our behalf and to celebrate the great victory his sacrificial death and resurrection accomplished over death and the Evil One. We listen to choirs sing mournful music about Jesus' death on the cross and triumphant melodies declaring that he arose. Certainly the birth, death, and resurrection of Jesus are events worthy of celebration. From beginning to end, the life of Jesus has set those of us who believe in him as Lord and Savior free from the fear of death, making possible our redemption and the inheritance of eternal life. The life of Jesus has shown us how to live as God's kingdom of priests in a broken world.

But the resurrection wasn't the end of Jesus' ministry on earth. He spent another forty days teaching his disciples about his kingdom and then ascended to heaven. So why do we not celebrate the ascension and Jesus' enthronement at God's right hand as King and Lord of all? Why is this miraculous event all but missing from our faith experience?

I dimly remember the Ascension Day worship services I attended when I was a child. The Protestant tradition I was part of held a special service to celebrate this event in Jesus' life, and my parents insisted that our family participate. Even then, more than five decades ago, the church was nearly empty. As the pastor read the story from the book of Acts, I imagined Jesus' disciples looking up as he disappeared into the clouds. I wasn't so sure I liked the part about Jesus returning in those clouds because I had many things I wanted to do first.

Since the time I left home to attend college, I have not attended an Ascension Day celebration. I do not recall ever hearing a sermon preached on this pivotal event in the ministry of Jesus or its impact on his followers. The closest thing I've heard to teaching about the ascension of Jesus is in the recitation of the Apostles' Creed: "he ascended into heaven and is seated at the right hand of God the Father Almighty; from there he shall come to judge the living and the dead."

Why do we downplay this event? Perhaps Jesus' ascension is more difficult for us to relate to experientially. Maybe, as I thought as a child, those of us who live in lands of opportunity and abundance are not all that eager for Jesus' return because we are quite comfortable where we are. Or, we may simply view Jesus' ascension as the way in which God ended Jesus' ministry on earth and believe it adds little spiritual benefit to what Jesus already accomplished by his sacrificial death and resurrection.

First-century followers of Jesus, however, had an entirely different view of the ascension's significance. Whereas the Text reveals little about Jesus' birth other than accounts in the gospels of Luke and Matthew, the reality of Jesus ascending to his Father to take his place at the Father's right hand is woven throughout the Christian Text. The ascended Jesus is mentioned six times, and his being "taken up" is mentioned seven times. Jesus' place at God's right hand is referred to six times in the Gospels, five times in the Acts of the Apostles, and eight times in the Epistles. In John's gospel, the reality of Jesus' return to his Father in heaven is woven throughout his comforting discourse during the Last Supper and his prayer for his disciples and himself as he faced the cross.

Two early believers, Peter and Stephen, mentioned Jesus' ascension in powerful speeches recorded in the Acts of the Apostles. Peter, on the Jewish day of Shavuot (Pentecost), explained the meaning of the sound of wind and the tongues of fire that the crowd experienced by declaring that Jesus' ascension and enthronement at God's right hand proved that God had crowned Jesus Lord and Messiah.[1] Stephen, on trial for his life, concluded his defense by dramatically describing his vision of Jesus at God's right hand.[2] After hearing this description of Jesus, the crowd stoned Stephen to death.

Whether Jew or Gentile, those who believed Jesus to be the promised Messiah (and those who did not) understood that the world had changed if Jesus indeed had ascended and was enthroned as Lord of all. In contrast, many followers of Jesus today do not recognize the significance of the ascension as it relates to Jesus' mission and the calling he gave to his disciples. Certainly it is biblical to believe the facts of the ascension, but it is not biblical enough. We also must recognize *what* it means. Consider how inspiring and instructive it would be if we were to reclaim the significance of Jesus' ascension and enthronement.[3]

The ascension declares that Jesus is enthroned in heaven as Lord of all — right now. Jesus' ascension is the basis for his claim to every square inch of God's world — all of creation and all human life. It is a powerful declaration that "Caesar" — whatever form he takes — isn't Lord. Jesus is! Satan wields great power, yet he ultimately is not in control — even in this world. Jesus alone is the ascended Lord, seated at God's right hand and in charge of all things right now and right here.

For those of us who follow Jesus, the ascension is a clarion call to living an obedient life in service to him, the King of kings. From his throne in heaven Jesus is in control on earth, and he commands his disciples to be living witnesses of his authority so that by obeying him in every part of life, his kingdom will come on earth as it is in heaven. Therefore, we must live in light of the ascension. It must shape our worldview and pattern for righteous living. Since Jesus is Lord, we must strive to do everything in obedience to his will and thereby display him in every sphere of human activity so that one day everything in this sin-filled world will be redeemed and restored.

Opening Thoughts (3 minutes)

The Very Words of God

> *When he had led them out to the vicinity of Bethany, he lifted up his hands and blessed them. While he was blessing them, he left them and was taken up into heaven. Then they worshiped him and returned to Jerusalem with great joy.*
>
> *Luke 24:50 – 52*

Think About It

When people are really excited or happy about something, they want to talk about it. They want to tell others. Astronomers can't wait to share their new discoveries. We want to tell our friends about the great book we just read. Parents want to talk about their children's achievements. Teens can't wait to Facebook, Instagram, or Tweet about everything that excites them. If you have any doubt about the human desire to share what excites us, try giving a seven-year-old a puppy and telling him or her to keep it a secret.

So, what excites you about your faith experience, and how eager are you to share it with others?

When, for example, was the last time you couldn't wait to tell someone about Jesus' ascension to heaven? Would you be able to explain how it changed your life and how important it is to the person you are talking to? Would you even know what to say about it?

Video Notes (30 minutes)

The message of the Arch of Titus

A first-century Roman-style tomb

Jesus rises from the dead

The "first fruits" rise from the dead

Forty days of teaching

The Ascension:
    The King is on his throne—go make disciples

The King in heaven rules on earth

Video Discussion (8 minutes)

1. When you saw the Arch of Titus, what did you realize about how powerful a message of conquest and domination it conveyed to the people of the Roman Empire?

    In what way did it help you to understand why the news of Jesus' resurrection and ascension was so significant for both Jews and Romans — the religious and political power brokers as well as ordinary people?

2. When you saw the first-century tomb, how did it inform your understanding of what Jesus' tomb may have been like? In what ways did it differ from what you expected?

3. What does the fact that Jesus taught about the kingdom of God during the forty days he was with his disciples after his resurrection indicate about its importance, and how well versed do you think we are when it comes to understanding the kingdom of God and our role in it?

4. In what ways do you view going and making disciples (also described as extending God's kingdom) differently when you realize that Jesus is on his throne in heaven and everything that is happening on earth is under his control?

DATA FILE
Mount of Olives

The Mount of Olives is a ridge more than two miles long with three summits, the highest of which is 2,900 feet above sea level. It was so named because of the extensive olive groves that at one time existed on its terraced western slope. The town of Bethany, home of Jesus' close friends Mary, Martha, and Lazarus, is on the eastern slope of the ridge at the edge of the Judah Wilderness that continues east to the Jordan valley and Dead Sea.

To the west of the Mount of Olives lies the Kidron valley, which separates the mountain from Mount Moriah on which David built Jerusalem. Solomon built the first temple at the highest point of Mount Moriah, which is 400 feet lower than the Mount of Olives. On the western slope of the Mount of Olives is the world's largest Jewish cemetery that dates back to before the Hebrews arrived. Still in use today, the graveyard is outside city limits so it does not violate Torah law forbidding burial within the city.   *(cont.)*

TAKEN FROM THE TEMPLE MOUNT, THIS PHOTO SHOWS THE RIDGE OF THE MOUNT OF OLIVES SEPARATING JERUSALEM FROM THE DESERT BEYOND. BETHANY IS LOCATED JUST OVER THE TOP OF THE RIDGE.

Visions of the prophets Ezekiel and Zechariah recorded in the Hebrew Bible describe the Mount of Olives as the place the Messiah will return when he judges the nations and restores the land to his people.[4] Perhaps this is why Jesus chose this ridge, in the vicinity of Bethany, for his ascension to the right hand of his Father. The testimony of the prophets, in addition to the fact that the Mount of Olives limestone is ideal for hewing burial chambers, is why Jewish people choose to be buried here in anticipation of the life to come.

Small Group Bible Discovery and Discussion (15 minutes)

Jesus' Ascension: Essential to Understanding Our Mission

The story of the ascension of Jesus receives little attention in Christian experience today — even on Ascension Day. We may profess our faith in the fact of Jesus' ascension and hold conferences to study biblical teaching about his return, but his ascent to his throne in heaven seems to have little significance to our community faith experience or to our daily walk as Jesus' disciples. To a large degree, we regard the ascension as simply God's confirmation that Jesus was the Messiah and that he completed his work on earth and went home!

While it is true the ascension does not add to our salvation or guarantee of eternal life, which were fully accomplished by Jesus' sacrificial death and resurrection, it is an unfortunate oversight to ignore it. To the first-century believers, Jesus' ascension was tremendously significant — even essential — to understanding Jesus' mission, their own calling as disciples, and what the message of God's kingdom would accomplish in their world. The ascension got people's attention. It was a radical and dangerous message to proclaim in the Roman Empire.

1. For what purposes did Jesus come to earth, and what did he accomplish? (See Matthew 9:35; John 3:16 – 17; 13:12 – 17; 17:1 – 4, 6, 20 – 23; Hebrews 2:9 – 11; 1 Peter 2:21 – 22.)

   In what ways does what Jesus accomplished help us better understand the mission God has given to his people and what it means to participate in extending the kingdom of heaven?

   What did Jesus teach as essential in order to participate in the kingdom of heaven? (See Matthew 4:17; 7:21.)

2. Jesus rose from the dead on the first day of the week, which
    that year was the Feast of Firstfruits. To whom did Jesus appear,
    and what did he teach during the forty days between his resur-
    rection and ascension? (See Acts 1:1 – 3; 1 Corinthians 15:3 – 8.)

3. Jesus gave his followers key instructions during the forty
    days he was with them after his resurrection.

    a. Read Matthew 28:10, 16 – 20 and discuss where Jesus
        told his disciples to go, what command he gave them,
        and why that command was significant in that location.

    b. Read Acts 1:4 – 5 and discuss what Jesus told his disciples
        to do and why it was important in order to fulfill the
        mission he had given them in Galilee.

    c. Read Acts 1:6 – 8 and discuss which command Jesus
        reminded his disciples of when they wanted to know
        when he would restore his kingdom. In what way was
        this an accurate answer?

FOR GREATER UNDERSTANDING

Following his resurrection, Jesus was seen in Galilee and in the vicinity of Jerusalem and the Mount of Olives. During the forty days before he ascended from the Mount of Olives, he taught his disciples about the kingdom of God.

In Matthew's gospel, Jesus instructed his disciples to go to the mountain in Galilee, where he gave them what we call the Great Commission. Then the disciples walked all the way back to Jerusalem where Jesus ascended to heaven. That walk was nearly 250 miles! Why walk that far for one teaching? Perhaps it is because Jesus wanted his disciples to be in Galilee, where he had taught and modeled how to be and make disciples. This would be a Jewish way to emphasize their mission of walking as Jesus walked and making disciples as he did.

4. From the beginning of his ministry, Jesus made it clear to his disciples that he would not always be with them physically on earth.

    a. Where did he say he would go? (See John 13:3; 14:1 – 4; 16:28.)

    b. What miraculous event did Jesus' disciples witness, and what impact did it have on them? (See Luke 24:50 – 51; Acts 1:9 – 11.)

    c. Jesus' disciples knew their Hebrew Bible well, so when Jesus ascended they likely remembered events, prophecies, and current experiences that enhanced their understanding of what they had witnessed. Read Exodus 24:15, Daniel 7:13 – 14, and Luke 24:4, and discuss the impact you think these memories would have had on their experience.

DID YOU KNOW?

Jewish tradition maintained that Levitical priests had the unique role in blessing God's people when they gathered for prayer or worship (Leviticus 9:22). The priests alone would raise their hands, which were believed to represent the wings of God, and pronounce the blessing of Aaron that God had given in the Torah (Numbers 6:22–27). Since Jesus was not of the tribe of Levi or from the family of Aaron, his act of raising his hands to bless his disciples is a clear claim to a distinct priesthood, which the writer of Hebrews indicates is the priesthood of Melchizedek, the priest who blessed Abraham (Genesis 14:18–20; Hebrews 5:5–10; 6:19–20; 7:1–28). Jews would understand Jesus' act of blessing his disciples as his claim to a Melchizedek priesthood.

Luke is the only Gospel writer who records Jesus raising his hands and blessing his disciples as he ascended to heaven. Interestingly, Luke began his book with the story of an old priest (Zechariah) who could not complete his task because of his loss of voice (in practice he would have followed the incense offering by joining the other priests in blessing the congregation; Luke 1:1–22) and ended his book with the Messiah, who claimed a new priesthood by his faithful obedience and was thereby able to bless the disciples.

Faith Lesson (3 minutes)

The ascension declared that Jesus is not only our Savior but has been enthroned in heaven at the right hand of the Father as Lord of all. This means that Jesus has been given all authority to rule in heaven and on earth. Although it is true that his reign will not be fully realized until he returns, his reign *has* begun. He — and no other — is Lord and King!

The reality of Jesus ruling in heaven should give us confidence and boldness in proclaiming through actions and words that Jesus — who completed his redemptive work — is Lord and King over all things. Our mission is to proclaim the reality of his kingdom and extend his reign through our own submission to the will of our King and his lordship. We must live with the conviction that our

world belongs entirely to God — all of it. In the words of Abraham
Kuyper, "There is not a square inch in the whole domain of our
human existence over which Christ, who is Sovereign over all, does
not cry, Mine!"[5]

Until Jesus returns to consummate his kingdom, his disciples are
commissioned to reclaim a broken world — its people as well as
every sphere in which we are involved, including business, politics,
art, sports, medicine, education, music, family, and more. They all
belong to God. As he gives us opportunities in his authority, by the
witness of our words and actions, we are called to reclaim everything one square inch at a time. Nothing belongs to the Evil One!

1. When Jesus' disciples left the Mount of Olives following his
   ascension, they were filled with joy. They were eager to do
   whatever he commanded them to do so that God's kingdom
   would come. What difference do you think the experience
   of Jesus' ascension made to them, and why?

   What difference does it make to you as you seek to follow
   him?

2. In Hebrews 12:2, Paul reminds us to fix "our eyes on Jesus,
   the pioneer and perfecter of faith. For the joy set before him
   he endured the cross, scorning its shame, and sat down at
   the right hand of the throne of God." We need this reminder
   because it is so easy for us to forget that Jesus is on the
   throne. In our own power, we are at risk for going through
   the motions of obedience — sincerely, yes — but lacking the
   confidence that Jesus is indeed on the throne now!

What may you have missed out on in your walk of faith by not understanding that Jesus is ruling *now*, that he is in charge, and that those who follow him serve a living, ruling King?

3. There is no doubt that we will face opposition and endure difficulties and persecution as we represent God's kingdom in a world that does not know him. In what ways does the fact that Jesus is seated at God's right hand, and has been given all authority to reign, encourage you to confront opposition with boldness, hope, and joy?

   What one thing are you eager to do — because Jesus is reigning — in order to claim one more square inch for the kingdom of God?

Closing (1 minute)

Read Luke 24:51 – 53 aloud together: "While he was blessing them, he left them and was taken up into heaven. Then they worshiped him and returned to Jerusalem with great joy. And they stayed continually at the temple, praising God."

Then pray, thanking Jesus that he came down from heaven to live among us and take our sinfulness on himself by dying on the cross.

Praise him for overcoming death and the Evil One so that we might
be restored to fellowship and life eternal with our Father in heaven.
Bless his name for being our example and teaching us to obey God
in all things so that we might be partners with him in restoring his
kingdom to its rightful place on earth. Rejoice in his ascension to
his throne in heaven where he reigns over all. May we be faithful in
obeying him as our almighty King and extending his reign on earth.
In Jesus' name, amen.

Memorize

> *While he was blessing them, he left them and was taken up into
> heaven. Then they worshiped him and returned to Jerusalem with great
> joy. And they stayed continually at the temple, praising God.*
>
> *Luke 24:51 – 53*

The Kingdom of Heaven Advances: Reclaiming What Belongs to God

In-Depth Personal Study Sessions

Study 1 | Jesus' Ascension in a Roman World

The Very Words of God

> *So do not be ashamed of the testimony about our Lord or of me his prisoner. Rather, join with me in suffering for the gospel, by the power of God. He has saved us and called us to a holy life — not because of anything we have done but because of his own purpose and grace. This grace was given us in Christ Jesus before the beginning of time, but it has now been revealed through the appearing of our Savior, Christ Jesus, who has destroyed death and has brought life and immortality to light through the gospel. And of this gospel I was appointed a herald and an apostle and a teacher. That is why I am suffering as I am. Yet this is no cause for shame, because I know whom I have believed, and am convinced that he is able to guard what I have entrusted to him until that day.*
>
> *2 Timothy 1:8 – 12*

Bible Discovery

The Kingdom of Heaven Reigns!

The right of ancient kings to rule was often rooted, as is Jesus' story, in a divine birth, an ascension, and enthronement in the heavens. Kings of Egypt, Persia, and Babylon, for example, claimed their deity and the divine right to rule because their fathers were said to have ascended to the gods. In fact, the Egyptian pyramids were built to help the spirit of the dead Pharaoh ascend and continue to influence life on earth through his successor who then became the "Son of God." By the time of Jesus, worship of the Roman emperor as divine had become a central feature of the Roman Empire's authority. This is the message of the Arch of Titus that depicts Titus ascending to heaven on the back of an eagle, indicating divine approval of his brother, Domitian, the emperor who built the arch.

At the time of Jesus' birth, the reigning emperor, Caesar Augustus, had been declared by the Roman Senate and Roman people to be the "Son of God" because of Julius Caesar's ascent to heaven and deification.[6] The calendar had been recreated to begin on the birthdate of Caesar Augustus. He was called the "Savior of the World" because he brought an age of peace and prosperity to his empire. His official title was "Lord and God." Clearly Caesar's kingdom was viewed as the sovereign kingdom in power when Luke wrote his account of the birth of Jesus.

To us, Luke's Christmas account (Luke 2:1 – 21) has become a beloved children's story, which is probably the reason we leave out the part about Herod killing the infants of Bethlehem. But in its time, Luke's Christmas story was a highly confrontational message regarding a fierce conflict between kingdoms — a clear affront to the Roman regime. Luke began his account of Jesus' birth with the words, "In those days Caesar Augustus issued a decree" (Luke 2:1). He then proceeded to undermine every claim that Caesar Augustus represented — Augustus, the most powerful man the world had ever known and the ruler whose decrees were never debatable!

In Imperial Roman communication, *Gospel*, *Lord*, and *Savior* were terms applied to the emperor alone. Luke revealed the startling reality that there was another Son of God who claimed to be Lord of all, and that King was a baby in a manger whose birth was heralded by angels. In contrast to the Roman gospel, Luke described the gospel of a Savior who would bring justice, peace, and blessing for all people — not just the rich, powerful, and privileged. In effect Luke states, through God's inspiration, that Jesus contradicts the false claims of the emperor who was not Lord, not God, and not Savior. Jesus challenged the Imperial gospel — a counterfeit of the Evil One himself — with the true gospel of God's kingdom. It's easy to see why the kingdom of Rome was on a collision course with the kingdom of heaven.

The conflict escalated even more after Jesus' ascension because, not unlike the pagan nations Israel knew previously, Imperial Rome also had ascension stories. Luke's ascension account and its consequences brought Jesus' followers into greater conflict with Roman rulers. If Jesus had truly ascended, he not only was the divine Savior but the true, sovereign Lord enthroned in heaven who rules over all of creation.[7] The implications of Jesus ascending and being enthroned in heaven as King of kings and Lord of lords caused Imperial Rome to label such claims treasonous.

Rome had done its best to kill Jesus and destroy his credibility and impact. Instead, the opposite happened. God had planned all along to use Jesus' death and resurrection for his glory and the redemption of humanity. God had planned all along to enthrone Jesus at his right hand. Jesus had brought the kingdom of heaven to earth, and Rome could do nothing to stop it.[8]

DATA FILE
Khirbet Midras — The Message of the Empty Tomb

The ruins of Khirbet Midras are located about thirty miles southwest of Jerusalem. The village is in the region of Israel called the *Shephelah*, the hilly country between the coastal plain and the Judea Mountains, near the cave of Adullam where David lived during his conflict with King Saul.[9] The village is about six acres in size and dates to approximately 1000 BC. It thrived during the Roman Era (63 BC – 300 AD). *(cont.)*

During the first- and second-century revolts against Rome, Zealot fighters used Khirbet Midras as a defensive location and hideout. They dug caves and extensive tunnels into the soft chalk rock under their homes to store food and weapons. Following the revolt, people hid in these caves for months and even years. Some of these caves can still be explored today. Among the remains are buildings, wine and olive presses, and caves for raising doves and pigeons. Some scholars think this site had a memorial church for the prophet Zechariah and may actually be the site of his tomb.

The tomb shown in the video is similar to the tomb of Jesus.[10] It was carved from the natural bedrock, which would be very expensive and implies ownership by a wealthy family. It had an open area in front of the tomb for mourners to gather, and where the soldiers likely stood guard. The opening to the tomb was sealed by a large rolling stone set into a channel, which the women who came to attend to Jesus' body were concerned about moving. The doorway into the mourning chamber and burial shelves was small so that a person would have to bend down to enter or look into it.

The empty tomb of Jesus, the risen Savior and Lord, sent shock waves through the religious and political establishment. The empty tomb meant the Jesus story wasn't over. God's kingdom had come, and death could not stop it. Jesus' resurrection was so threatening that those in power conspired to suppress the truth. Even before Jesus ascended to heaven, where he was enthroned as Lord of all, his message posed a powerful threat to the kingdom of this world.

1. After Jesus' resurrection, what "kingdom" did Jesus teach about? (See Acts 1:3, 8.)

What mission did he give his followers that would upset the status quo of the kingdom of Imperial Rome?

How significant do you think it is that Jesus ascended right after he restated their mission?

2. God's kingdom, or the kingdom of heaven, is not about a place. It is about people recognizing God's redeeming power at work, professing their belief that he is King, and accepting his reign in their lives by obedience to his commands. Part of Jesus' ministry on earth was to show his people how to extend the reign of his kingdom by obeying him.

    Consider how the message of the kingdom of heaven was conveyed and the impact it had on extending God's reign (which, of course, would be a threat to Rome's reign) in each of the following examples.

    a. By John the Baptist, Matthew 3:1 – 6

    b. By Jesus, Matthew 9:35 – 38

   c. By the message Jesus assigned to his disciples, Matthew 10:1 – 8

   d. By Philip, Acts 8:12

   e. By Paul, Acts 19:8 – 10

3. In Isaiah 43:9 – 13, what did the prophet say about the mission of being God's witnesses to the nations? How certain do you think the disciples were that Jesus was in heaven, ruling as King over all the earth, and how might that assurance have influenced how they carried out their mission?

DATA FILE
The Message of the Triumphal Arch

It was common Roman practice to build triumphal arches to glorify their self-proclaimed divine emperors. The most famous of these arches is the Arch of Titus in Rome, which portrays his victory over the Jewish rebellion in 70 AD. Made of marble, the arch is 50 feet high, 45 feet wide, and 15 feet deep and is surrounded by columns with Corinthian capitals. Domitian raised this arch after the death of his brother, Emperor Titus, in 81 AD. The arch honored both Titus and his father, Vespasian, for their victories during the Jewish Revolt that ended with the conquest of Jerusalem and the destruction of the temple.

CARVINGS ON THE ARCH DEPICT THE TRIUMPHAL VICTORY PROCESSION IN ROME IN 71 AD IN WHICH THE TABLE, MENORAH, AND SILVER TRUMPETS FROM GOD'S TEMPLE ARE PARADED BEFORE THE CROWD TO BE DISPLAYED IN VESPASIAN'S TEMPLE OF PEACE. THE CARVING ON THE INSIDE PEAK OF THE ARCH DEPICTS ROME'S ASCENSION STORY — EMPEROR TITUS RIDING AN EAGLE TO TAKE HIS PLACE AT THE RIGHT HAND OF JUPITER IN HEAVEN. THE ARCH MADE A STRONG STATEMENT ABOUT THE KINGDOM OF ROME AND ITS DEIFIED EMPEROR.

POINT TO PONDER

King Herod built three temples to Caesar Augustus in Israel: Caesarea on the coast, Sebastia (formerly named Samaria), and Omrit just south of Caesarea Philippi. It is amazing to realize that when Peter confessed, "You are the Messiah, the Son of the living God"[11] at Caesarea Philippi, he was less than two miles from the temple declaring Caesar to be the divine Son of God!

In the Roman world, the Christian message was not simply a new way of being religious or getting to the life to come. In the context of first-century political and religious reality, the Christian message radically challenged the status quo of Imperial Rome—the authority, worldview, and belief system of a kingdom that demanded total allegiance. Many of Jesus' disciples who witnessed his ascension had also heard Peter's profession. They, too, proclaimed the reality that Jesus alone is God. Like Peter, they faced Rome's brutal response and paid for it with their lives.

Reflection

Jesus' ascension and enthronement at God's right hand provides the basis for all followers of Jesus to believe, live out, and proclaim the truth that he is Savior and Lord. The ascension declared that Jesus is Lord of all. As his followers, we are to proclaim the good news of his salvation and demonstrate his lordship by doing his will and thereby extending his reign. We are partners with God in extending his reign until all things are under his feet and every knee shall bow and tongue confess that he is Lord of all.[12]

Jesus called his disciples to be witnesses who testified in life and in word that he had ascended and been given all authority in heaven and on earth, and they were called to be disciples who made disciples. They were to be like Jesus in how they announced and advanced his kingdom. They were to love their enemies and pray for those who persecuted them. They were to care for the poor, the sick, and the lonely. They were to seek the lost. They were to live sacrificially for others, to serve and not to be served. In all things they were to imitate Jesus, knowing that while his kingdom was *in* this world, it did not come *from* this world. Jesus' kingdom was not a kingdom of political or economic power like the kingdoms of this world; it was a kingdom of justice and righteousness.

Whereas Rome extended its reign through raw, oppressive power, Jesus gave his disciples the mission of proclaiming and extending God's reign by *hallowing* his name, which means to bring honor and increase his reputation so that others would praise him also. The mission required obedient submission to doing God's will on earth so that his kingdom would come on earth as it is already in heaven.

> Reread Jesus' prayer in Matthew 6:9 – 13. In what ways has this study broadened your understanding of this prayer and your commitment to live by it?

> As you consider what is required to *hallow* God's name and extend his kingdom on earth through faithful obedience to his commands and loving imitation of how Jesus obeyed the Father, what difference does it make to you that Jesus is the ascended and enthroned King of heaven, who at this very moment rules over all?

The kingdom of heaven, as it was lived out and taught by the early believers, was such a contrast to the kingdom of Rome that people wanted to be part of it.

> How does Isaiah 52:7 describe the mission of followers of Jesus to proclaim the good news of the kingdom of heaven?

In what ways are people in our world today hungry for that good news?

What are some practical actions we can take to share the true gospel of our Messiah and represent a very different kingdom than any that exist in our world today?

What is your commitment to accepting God's reign in your life and living out the mission that Jesus' ascension declared: that Jesus is not only Savior but has ascended and been made Lord of all?

Memorize

> *How beautiful on the mountains are the feet of those who bring good news, who proclaim peace, who bring good tidings, who proclaim salvation, who say to Zion, "Your God reigns!"*
>
> **Isaiah 52:7**

Study 2 | The Ascension in Historical Context

The Very Words of God

> *But Stephen, full of the Holy Spirit, looked up to heaven and saw the glory of God, and Jesus standing at the right hand of God. "Look," he said, "I see heaven open and the Son of Man standing at the right hand of God."*
>
> **Acts 7:55 – 56**

Bible Discovery

A Foundation for Accepting Jesus' Ascension

Whether or not they believed Jesus was the promised Messiah, the Jewish people had a significant foundation for the ascension in their Text and in the faith experience of those who had gone before them. The ascent, or journey "up" to meet with God is not uncommon in the Hebrew Bible.[13] Moses climbed Mount Sinai to meet with God and on the day of his death ascended Mount Nebo.[14] At the end of his faithful service to the Lord, Elijah ascended to heaven after the chariot of fire, representing God's presence, came down to meet him. The book of Daniel described a figure, the Son of Man, seated at God's right hand with authority over all the kingdoms of this world.

Clearly the paradigm of an ascent to God — whether to be with God in heaven, receive God's stamp of approval on a life of faithful service, or receive revelation from God — was well known to biblically literate Jewish people. They also recognized being seated at the right of God as a sign of authority to rule on earth. So Jesus' ascension and enthronement boldly declared to the Jews that God approved his claims and mission.

The Bible makes clear that Jesus, God's Son, came to earth to redeem lost humanity and would return to his Father.[15] He became human so that by his sacrificial death those who believe would find forgiveness for their rebellion against God. Having completed his redemptive work — to defeat the Evil One and release humankind from the bondage of sin — Jesus, the true Son of God, returned to the Father. His ascension underscores God's desire to "descend" and be present among and within his people. God was present in the tabernacle and the temple, and lived among his people in the person of Jesus.

Although first-century, scripturally literate Jews likely were surprised by Jesus' resurrection — and no doubt by his ascension — the idea was familiar to them. Although the purposes of such journeys (and revelation) varied, they provided a greater understanding of the meaning and purpose of Jesus' ascension. Let's explore several of these historical events and learn more about how the Jews of Jesus' day would have understood ascension.

1. The book of Daniel is a true story about righteous Jews liv-
    ing in captivity in Babylon. It was quite popular in Jesus' day,
    likely because of its stories about God delivering his people
    when they faced persecution for their faithfulness to him.
    It would have been an encouragement to Jewish people
    who faced Rome's oppression. (See Daniel 2:17 – 19, 36 – 37,
    44 – 47; 5:22 – 31; 7:13 – 14.)

    a. What did Daniel testify to the Babylonian kings (and to
        his readers) about the God of heaven and who is really in
        control of the kingdoms of this world?

    b. How does a true picture of the God of heaven help us to
        comprehend the significance of Jesus' ascension and his
        role?

2. On several occasions, God called Moses to ascend Mount
    Sinai in order to meet with him. (See Exodus 19:3 – 6, 9, 20;
    24:9 – 18.)

    a. For what important purposes did Moses experience the
        Lord's presence?

b. What occurred while Moses was with God on the mountain? (See Exodus 32:1 – 6.)

c. Israel was God's chosen bride, so when Israel was unfaithful to God,[16] it was as if Israel chose another lover over God. What might we learn from this regarding Jesus' reminders to his disciples to remain faithful to their mission after his ascension?

d. How was God's presence made visible on the mountain when Moses met with God? (See Exodus 19:9; 24:15 – 18.)

e. Since Jesus' disciples were likely aware of the details of Moses' interaction with God at Mount Sinai, what might they have concluded about the way Jesus ascended? (See Acts 1:9 – 11.)

3. How did God demonstrate his mercy and reward Elijah's faithful, obedient "walk" of service to him? In what way do you think Jesus' ascension validates his faithful life of righteous obedience and his completion of his redemptive task? (See 2 Kings 2:1 – 12.)

4. Isaiah did not literally ascend to meet with God, but what experience did the prophet have in God's presence, how did he respond, and what did God do for him? (See Isaiah 6:1 – 7.)

    What question did God then ask, and what was Isaiah's response? (See Isaiah 6:8 – 9.)

    Following his death and resurrection, what similar mission did Jesus give to his disciples (who likely knew Isaiah's experiences) before ascending to the Father's right hand? (See Matthew 28:18 – 20.)

DID YOU KNOW?

After Jesus ascended to heaven, some of his followers also had experiences in the presence of God, whether through vision or supernatural intervention. Apparently Paul described being taken up to heaven to receive revelation from God,[17] although he presents it as if it were someone else. This gave him a taste of God's unimaginable and inexplicable greatness, adding to his boldness and passion for his God-given mission. John, too, received revelation of what the future held for the community of Jesus-followers. His vision of the kingdom of God in heaven was given to encourage believers who would be facing great persecution.[18]

FOR GREATER UNDERSTANDING
Israel's Experience as a Model for Jesus' Experience

Jesus' path to the cross and the events leading up to and including his ascension followed the paradigm of Israel's history and calendar. This historical model was woven into the life and faith experience of all faithful Jews at the time. It helped them to anticipate and understand the message and meaning of Jesus' life and ministry.

As you review the chart that follows, please be aware that scholars debate the exact date of Jesus' last Passover, crucifixion, and resurrection. The goal here is not to present evidence for the exact day or date of these events (I provide support for the actual day they fulfill in earlier sessions). The intent is to show how Jesus' actions are set in the template of Israel's experience, which deepens our understanding of his mission and highlights the importance of Israel's experience.

Israel's Experience	Jesus' Experience
Israel chose Passover lamb on tenth day,[19] put blood on door, ate Seder meal on eve of fourteenth day,[20] ate Passover on fourteenth day, left Egypt on fourteenth day.	Jesus entered city on tenth day as lamb of God,[21] ate Seder and instituted Lord's Supper with Israel,[22] ate Passover on fourteenth day, shed blood as God's lamb on fourteenth day.

(cont.)

Israel's Experience	Jesus' Experience
First daily sacrifice made in temple for Israel at mid morning—third hour.[23]	Jesus crucified at third hour.[24]
Second daily sacrifice made in temple for Israel at mid afternoon—ninth hour.	Jesus died at ninth hour.[25]
Unleavened Bread Feast day after Passover. Tradition of prayer for bread from the ground.[26]	Jesus buried as Unleavened Bread Feast begins.[27]
Feast of Firstfruits two days after Passover; offering of first ripe barley harvest made in temple.[28]	Jesus resurrected on Feast of Firstfruits as the first fruit.[29]
Israel took approximately forty days to arrive at Sinai.[30]	Jesus taught his disciples about the kingdom of heaven[31] for forty days after Passover;[32] showed himself to crowds.[33]
Moses went up Mount Sinai to meet with God.[34]	Jesus went to the vicinity of Bethany, eastern slope of Mount of Olives, to be with his Father[35]; Jesus raised his hands, blessed disciples,[36] and was taken up to heaven[37] in a cloud—a common symbol for divine presence[38]—hidden from their sight.
About ten days later was Shavuoth (Pentecost) and the first giving of the Ten Commandments when God gave Moses the tablets and Israel worshiped the golden calf. God commanded the Levites to bring judgment on the guilty and about 3,000 died.[39]	Ten days later on Shavuoth, Jesus sent his Spirit on the new community and about 3,000 believed.[40]

Reflection

Jesus brought his disciples back to Jerusalem, where he gave them their final kingdom lessons. He commanded them to wait in Jerusalem until they received the Spirit the Father had promised. These ordinary young men were to become his witnesses — of the way he lived, the lessons he taught, his redemptive death and resurrection, and the kingdom of God. Although they wanted a calendar, he gave them an agenda: to go and bear witness. Then he led them out to the vicinity of Bethany, the eastern slope of the Mount of Olives, and ascended to heaven.

The ascension powerfully declared that Jesus is not only Savior but Lord of all. Jesus' disciples recognized that their mission (and ours today) was not only to tell people how to have a personal relationship with God through Jesus but to extend God's reign by living obediently in all areas of life, so that his kingdom would come as his will was done. That proclamation of God's reign is a key part of the gospel message. Although Jesus' reign will not be fully realized until his return, the kingdom of God has come and his reign has begun.

The mission of Israel was to obey God and thereby display him as he is and extend his reign in their world. Read Exodus 19:3 – 8; 24:3, 7; and Deuteronomy 5:27.

> To what extent do you think the disciples' heritage of being God's people — a people with a mission to obey God in all of life so that God's name would be made known in the world — influenced their understanding of the agenda Jesus gave them before he ascended to heaven?

> In what ways are Jesus' disciples our heritage, helping us to understand and know how to fulfill the mission Jesus has given all of his followers today?

What kinds of things hinder you from representing and proclaiming the kingdom of God and extending it by your obedience to the will of the King — Jesus Christ?

Memorize

*But you are a chosen people, a royal priesthood, a holy nation, God's
special possession, that you may declare the praises of him who called
you out of darkness into his wonderful light. Dear friends, I urge you,
as foreigners and exiles, to abstain from sinful desires, which wage war
against your soul. Live such good lives among the pagans that, though
they accuse you of doing wrong, they may see your good deeds and
glorify God on the day he visits us.*

1 Peter 2:9 – 12

Study 3 | Jesus' Ascension: Our Call to Discipleship

The Very Words of God

*Since, then, you have been raised with Christ, set your hearts on things
above, where Christ is, seated at the right hand of God. Set your minds
on things above, not on earthly things.*

Colossians 3:1 – 2

Bible Discovery

Go! Take Back What Belongs to Me!

The ascension declares that Jesus is Lord of the entire world. As his followers, we are to announce this truth and demonstrate and bring the
reign of the kingdom of God into our lives and extend it into our world

one square inch at a time. This means we must renounce all other ways of life. Our mission is to be like Jesus so that our lives will illustrate the nature of his kingdom and we will be living witnesses of the very nature of the King of kings and Lord of lords. We must do more than tell people about Jesus, as essential as that is. We must demonstrate what Jesus is like by being obedient in every dimension of life. This is what enables people to see and desire the *shalom* that results from doing God's will. We must be active participants in restoring God's lost children to the Father's house — *beth ab* — and in raising up disciples who also believe in and imitate this radically different King.

Perhaps one reason the community of Jesus seems to have decreasing influence today is that we often *talk about* Jesus' lordship rather than *demonstrating it* in everything we do. Our record in marriage, honesty, gossip, racism, care for the poor and those in need, addiction — you can add so much more to this list — is not all that different from people who do not follow Jesus. How can we proclaim that Jesus is King when we, his own people, do not submit to his authority? We must not be satisfied with simply turning to Jesus in faith and "being saved." We must strive to do what we can so that his kingdom will come on earth as it is in heaven.

Where would we be if the early Christians had kept Jesus out of their financial life, their sex life, their social life, their athletics, and their marriages? It would be as if Jesus' ascension never happened. The pagans would have concluded that Mammon was the god of money, Aphrodite the goddess of erotic love, and Mars the god of violence and power — and that Jesus had no place in these or any other areas of life! But the ascension says Jesus is Lord of all! If we understand the ascension, we begin to understand what it means to live that way.

The ascension declared to the disciples and Luke's readers that Jesus is the true King of Israel and therefore the Lord of the world. Jesus ascended to heaven, but this did not make him uninvolved or irrelevant to what was happening on earth. Instead, Jesus was put in charge of everything! Empowered by his Spirit, informed and guided by his teaching and example, his disciples became the ambassadors not of a crucified prophet but of a reigning king. Despite claims of others to the contrary, Jesus alone is Savior, Lord, and King. The gospel message was great news, and it changed the world.

1. What is God's overarching desire for those who have experi-
    enced the redeeming love of Jesus, the King and Lord of all?
    (See 1 John 2:3 – 6.)

2. As you read the following passages, what do you learn about
    God's purpose, calling, and empowerment for every disciple
    of Jesus who acknowledges him as Lord and King?

    a. Matthew 28:18 – 20

    b. Mark 13:9 – 11

    c. Luke 2:25 – 32

    d. Luke 24:46 – 48

e.   1 Peter 2:4 – 12

FOR GREATER UNDERSTANDING
Luke and the Acts of the Apostles

The community of Jesus has always believed that Luke wrote two books or maybe one book in two parts — the gospel of Luke and the Acts of the Apostles. The ascension story links the two books together. The gospel of Luke concludes with Jesus blessing his disciples and being "taken up" to be enthroned at the right hand of the Father with complete authority over all things.

The ascension is also the beginning of the mission of the disciples — now called apostles or official messengers of the kingdom of heaven and its enthroned King. The ascension is the foundation that provided the message, the courage, and the mission they would live out with amazing results. Today it remains the basis for the message and mission that disciples of Jesus are to live out throughout the world.

With Jesus' ascension and enthronement as the starting point, the book of Acts is divided into two parts. The first half (through chapter 12) follows Jesus' disciples and first believers in declaring that Jesus is Israel's Messiah and therefore their King (2:22 – 37). The first half ends with Herod, the Edomite and so-called king of the Jews, recognizing the threat that followers of Jesus posed to his authority — much as his grandfather had recognized the announcement of Jesus' birth as a threat. So Herod arrested and killed James, and intended to do the same to Peter, but God intervened and Peter escaped. Herod later held an audience with his subjects who praised him as God and Lord, but because he refused to accept the lordship of Jesus, God struck him down (Acts 12). Jesus alone is the King of Israel.

(cont.)

The second half of Acts follows the travels of Saul—Paul as he chose to call himself. Its theme focuses on Jesus as not only Israel's Messiah but Lord and King of the entire world,[41] just as the Hebrew Bible predicted. Not surprisingly, the economic, political, moral, and religious implications for Rome and for Israel's religious leaders caused serious opposition.[42] So, the book ends with Paul in Rome waiting to share the good news of Jesus with Caesar.[43] Perhaps Caesar, like Herod, had an opportunity to submit to King Jesus. Perhaps Luke's readers understood Nero's forced suicide shortly after Paul's death to be God's reaction to Nero's refusal to accept the ascended and enthroned Jesus as his King.

3. With great boldness and conviction, Jesus' disciples displayed and declared the message of the kingdom of God. Just as the prophets had foretold, God created among them a community that served him as their King and had a powerful influence on their world. Take some time and read Acts 3, 4, and 5:17 – 42. (And feel free to keep reading! It is a powerful story you won't want to put down.) As you read, take note of what you see in these Jesus-followers' example and how it instructs and encourages you in your own walk of faith. Consider at least the following in your study:

   a. The power and courage they had in carrying out the mission

   b. What troubled the religious establishment, and the disciples' boldness in replying to all charges

c. Their faith that Jesus was 100 percent in charge

d. Their compassion for those in need

e. Their unstoppable testimony

f. The conviction and power of a supportive community of believers

DATA FILE
True Discipleship

A disciple of Jesus learns to walk with God, or to live a godly life, by imitating his teacher, the rabbi. Jesus' disciple, John, expressed it this way: "Whoever claims to live in him must walk as Jesus did."[44] The disciples' mission was to imitate Jesus in every way and teach others by word and life to imitate Jesus, too. If the disciples were faithful in their walk, *their* disciples would be imitating Jesus by imitating them. Or, as Paul wrote, "Follow my example, as I follow the example of Christ."[45]

Jesus had earlier described their mission as being "the salt of the earth" and "the light of the world."[46] He explained that they should live a life of doing good works so that people in their spheres of influence would see and learn to know God. In the disciples' prayer, Jesus taught them to "hallow" God's name. This concept — *kiddush ha shem* in Hebrew — meant to give honor to God and to increase his reputation so others would honor and praise him.

Thus the disciples received the same mission as Israel had before them and were called to continue that mission. Israel was to make God's name known,[47] be a light to the Gentiles,[48] and was never to profane his name (the opposite of *kiddush ha shem* or *hillul ha shem*). The disciples were not only to proclaim the Lord Jesus to pagan nations but were to demonstrate who he was and what following him looked like. They were to be a kingdom of priests — submitting to God's reign in order to demonstrate what God is like.

Reflection

If Jesus' ascension and enthronement at the right hand of the Father is given its rightful emphasis in our faith, we must become more than people who believe Jesus ascended and, after preparing a place for us, will return to take us with him. We must recognize the ascension for what it is: a declaration that Jesus is Lord of all right now and that he commands his disciples to be living witnesses of that authority so that as we imitate him, his kingdom will come on earth as it is in heaven. This means:

- We must live as disciples, or imitators, of Jesus — our model of how to apply his authority to every area of life — and renounce all other ways of life.

- We must be more than "preachers" offering a religious experience to those who do not know our Lord. We must be obedient, godly representatives of the reigning King, whose words and actions invite others to leave their brokenness and receive the *shalom* that comes when God reigns.

- We must establish and be actively involved in communities of people who are faithful to the ascended King and will support one another in obedience to him. These communities — church communities, families, Bible study groups, dorm mates, fellow employees, groups of neighbors — must be a living testimony to the ascension's reality that Jesus is Lord and God!

- We must be people who willingly enter the chaos of the lives of people around us who remain in bondage, and bring redemption — purchased by Jesus' death and resurrection, and guaranteed by his ascension — that will restore lost people in a broken world to wholeness and *shalom*.

Jesus is not away being King in a distant place where he does not care about how we live, how we care for others, how we respond to temptations. He is King of all *now* — in our lives and in the world.

> Do we truly believe that God calls us and will empower us — to display God to others in every single moment of our lives? Why or why not?

> In what practical ways can we invite God into every corner of our lives — our successes and failures? Into our goals and dreams?

Paul, in Philippians 2:9 – 11 and Ephesians 1:18 – 23, dramatically declares Jesus to be Lord and King over all things, based on his redemptive death on the cross and his ascension and enthronement at the right hand of the Father.

What does it mean to you that the power of the resurrection and ascension is available to us as we serve and obey him?

What have you experienced of God's hope and power?

What confidence does Jesus' ascension provide as you try to live in a world still full of chaos that in many senses appears to be a world out of control?

God invites us to choose him as Lord of all, to obey his will as our King, and thereby extend his earthly reign. The question for us is, will we choose him?

Are you willing to become part of his redemptive presence in the world in order to reclaim his lost children from the Evil One's bondage?

In which specific ways are you willing to take back God's domain one inch at a time?

Memorize

> *I pray that the eyes of your heart may be enlightened in order that you may know the hope to which he has called you, the riches of his glorious inheritance in his holy people, and his incomparably great power for us who believe. That power is the same as the mighty strength he exerted when he raised Christ from the dead and seated him at his right hand in the heavenly realms, far above all rule and authority, power and dominion, and every name that is invoked, not only in the present age but also in the one to come.*

> **Ephesians 1:18–21**

PENTECOST: GOD CHANGED HIS ADDRESS

There are striking similarities between the beginning of the Bible's great story and the last chapters of its final book. Both describe a new heaven and earth, each having a garden in which the tree of life bears fruit. Most important, God is personally present among his people who live there.

From the beginning, God acted to make himself known through the witness of his magnificent creation and to live in intimate relationship with the human image bearers he created.[1] He entrusted the care of his magnificent creation to our human ancestors, Adam and Eve, the crown of his creation. And he was present with them — not just appearing to them on occasion as he did with Abraham, Isaac, Jacob, Joseph, Moses, and Elijah — but in close, personal relationship. In a sense, there was no separation between heaven and earth; they met in the Garden of Eden. God was present and shared in a wonderfully intimate relationship wherever his human friends were. God *walked* (a Hebrew metaphor meaning "lived") with them in the Garden of Eden. Where they lived, he lived.[2]

Then, enticed by the Evil One, Adam and Eve rebelled against God and radically changed their intimate friendship with him. The holy God could not be present with that which is sinful and unclean. Although in one sense he was (and still is) present everywhere, in another sense he had to separate himself from them and their sinful descendants. Heaven and earth were separated by a great gulf.

Yet even after his rebellious humans sinned, God continued to demonstrate his desire to renew his intimate presence with them.

The Text describes him as "looking," "speaking," and "appearing" to them. Even more remarkable, God chose them to be his partners in bringing his presence into and redeeming their broken world.

- First God chose to redeem individuals and worked in and through them so that those in spiritual darkness would come to know his presence.

- Then God chose a nation, Israel, to be his kingdom of priests,[3] a community that would put him on display by their words and actions and thereby bear his presence to their pagan neighbors.

- Time passed and God chose to become human in his Son, Jesus, and literally lived in community with the Jewish people of that day. Even then God had not finished his great plan to restore the intimacy he experienced with human beings in the Garden.

- After Jesus ascended, the disciples returned to Jerusalem to wait for God's Spirit. Ten days later, during the festival of Shavuoth (Pentecost), God's Spirit fell on the community of Jesus-followers. Joyfully they dispersed around the Roman world, not only sharing what God had accomplished through Jesus' redemptive teaching and actions but bearing God's very presence with them. Now the intimacy between God and his human creation could be restored anywhere and for anyone.

The mission to make God's name known and be a light to the nations — the mission God originally gave to the people of Israel — is now extended to followers of Jesus.[4] They are to be "salt" and "light" to the nations and to hallow God's name by living in a godly way so that other people will come to know the God of heaven through them. They are to do his will so that his kingdom will come. They are to be his witnesses in word and life, making disciples who will imitate Jesus as they see his community doing.

From this perspective, the story of Pentecost is as central to the biblical story as God's covenant with Israel at Mount Sinai. The inspired writers make this connection in many ways, including the fact that both events happened during the same festivals and took place on the "Mountain of God." Let's explore the implications of God sending his Spirit to live within and among the community of God's redeemed people.

Opening Thoughts (3 minutes)

The Very Words of God

> *Look! God's dwelling place is now among the people, and he will dwell with them. They will be his people, and God himself will be with them and be their God.*

> *Revelation 21:3*

Think About It

Often we think about our relationship with God in terms of whether or not we have been "saved" or "redeemed." We speak of having a right relationship with God and feeling his presence in our lives, but what do we really mean when we say those things?

Is our relationship with God a box we check "yes" or "no" and then continue our lives as we always have, or is it a personal, interactive relationship that is essential to our everyday life?

Is God's presence a good feeling of spiritual contentment, or is it a relationship that directs and empowers our path through life?

We often are self-focused when we speak of our relationship with God — what we feel, what we want, what it means to us — as if we are the only one involved. How much thought do we give to what God wants in a relationship with us?

Video Notes (30 minutes)

The temple mount in Jerusalem—the place where Jesus walked

The Mountain of God

    God speaks at Mount Sinai—obedience is the mission

    Mount Moriah—the house of the Lord, or the Father's house

The Father's house—*beth ab*

    Where God's presence lives among his people

    Where God's lost children are redeemed and restored

The person of Jesus—where heaven and earth meet

God moves into the "house" of his people

Video Discussion (7 minutes)

1. When you viewed what remains of the Temple Mount in Jerusalem and saw the massive size of its stones and considered the events that occurred (and still do occur) there, what do you think it must have been like to worship God at the temple during the time of Jesus?

2. What new understanding have you gained about how the Jewish people viewed the temple and why the religious leaders were so upset when they thought Jesus spoke of destroying the temple, the place where God's presence lived and where they received forgiveness for their sins?

3. God has a long history of creating opportunities to bring
    heaven and earth together so that he could meet and live
    among his people — in the Garden of Eden, at Mount Sinai,
    in the tabernacle, in the temple in Jerusalem, and now in his
    people.

    a. How significant is it to you that you, if you are a follower
        of Jesus, are part of that long history of being God's pres-
        ence on earth?

    b. How does that realization change your perspective on
        what it means to be God's witness in the world, to be
        the presence of God on earth in order to help redeem
        and restore God's lost children to *beth ab,* to the Father's
        house?

4. How aware have you been of what God has been doing —
    since the beginning of humanity — to have genuine, intimate
    relationships with the people he created?

    In what ways has this video given you a greater appreciation
    for the commitment and effort God has expended to restore
    you and others to relationship with him, or helped broaden

your understanding of what God wants in a relationship with you?

5. To what extent do you agree that we tend to think of the gift of the Holy Spirit as something God gives us just for our encouragement and comfort? In what ways does this perspective limit our ability to be God's message in our world, to be the place where heaven and earth meet?

To what extent do you agree with the statement that having compassion for the poor provides powerful evidence that the Spirit of God dwells within us?

DATA FILE
What Is Redemption?

The Hebrew word translated *redemption* originally did not have the spiritual connotations we associate with it. It simply meant to deliver people—to pay their debts, free them from bondage or slavery, and restore them to their family and community. Redemption of lost or marginalized family members was the responsibility of the patriarch or senior male in each family or *beth ab*.[5] God used the word to describe his program of seeking and restoring his alienated human children who rebelled against him and were under bondage to their sinful nature. God acted to pay their debt (because of sin), set them free, and restore them to relationship with him and to his community.

God first redeemed individuals such as Abraham, Isaac, Jacob, Joseph, and Moses. With their help, he raised up his chosen people — Israel — and redeemed them. He then called them to be his instrument of redemption to all nations. When Jesus came and identified himself as Messiah, God's redeemer, the work God called Israel to do in partnership with him truly reached all nations. God continues to use his partners today — Jews and Gentiles who have been grafted into the Jewish tree — who have been redeemed through the redemptive work of Jesus and commissioned to use God's resources to bring the good news of Jesus to all people. As Jesus-followers, we too are called to be the community through which God redeems his lost children.[6]

Small Group Bible Discovery and Discussion (16 minutes)

God Meets the Hebrews at the Mountain of God!

In most Near Eastern religions of biblical times, mountains were viewed as sacred places where the worlds of the gods and humans met. The mountain heights reached up to where the gods were believed to reside, and because few people reached the mountain summits, they seemed mysterious and otherworldly. Sacred mountains, and more local manifestations of this belief called "high places," were common in Egyptian, Babylonian, Canaanite, and Hittite cultures.

It seems that God chose to use the common understanding of gods metaphorically meeting people on sacred mountains to reveal his desire to break down the barrier of separation between himself and humanity and to restore his people to intimate communion with him. He met his people on mountains and even designated two mountains as the "Mountain of the Lord." If heaven[7] is thought of as being in God's presence and earth as the dwelling place of sinful humans, there is a sense in which heaven and earth meet on the Mountain of the Lord.[8]

What took place between God and his people at the Mountain of God — sometimes called Mount Horeb and other times Mount Sinai — played a pivotal role in ancient Israel's history. Events there formed Israel's relationship with God, giving them their mission and shaping their identity as a people. At the Mountain of God, the holy God — Creator and Lord of the universe — actually gave his people opportunities to experience his presence in rich and varied ways. Let's explore some of their experiences of God's presence at the Mountain of God and consider the nature and impact it had on their lives.

1. Moses was alone, out in the desert tending sheep when God first appeared to him. Read about his encounter with God in Exodus 3:1 – 12.

    a. Where and how did the Lord's presence appear to him?

    b. How did God make himself known to Moses, and what did he reveal of his character and love for the people he had created?

    c. What kind of a relationship did God propose to Moses, and what was God's commitment to that relationship?

2. Who did God send to meet Moses at the Mountain of God? What did they do together, and how did it affect the relationship other people had with God? (See Exodus 4:27 – 31.)

3. After God delivered the Hebrews from the Egyptians, they traveled through the desert and camped at the foot of the Mountain of God, just as God had promised Moses they would. While the people were encamped there, God called Moses to meet with him on the mountain where he revealed the intimate relationship[9] he wanted to have with his people and gave them the mission to draw others who did not know God into relationship with him.

   a. What kind of relationship did God want to have with his people, and what impact was that relationship to have on others? (See Exodus 19:3 – 6.)

   b. In what way did God reveal himself to his people, and what role did Moses have in that interaction? (See Exodus 19:9, 16 – 19.)

    c.   How did the code of conduct God provided for his people not only extend his desire to reign in every aspect of their lives but enable them to display him — the awesome, true God — to others and call him *their* God? (See Exodus 20:1 – 17.)

4.   Who went up to meet God on the mountain to ratify the covenant — God's eternal relationship with his people — and what did they do to prepare for going up to meet with God? (See Exodus 24:1 – 11.)

For how long did Moses stay on the mountain, and what provision did God specify so that his presence would be with his people continually? (See Exodus 24:13 – 25:8.)

While Moses was on the mountain, how did Israel violate their relationship with God, and what was his response? (See Exodus 32:1 – 10.)

What profound truth did Moses realize concerning Israel's need for a relationship with God and its impact on people who did not know God? (See Exodus 33:15 – 23.)

5. Whenever Moses met with God and spoke with him one-on-one, what would result from his being in God's presence? (See Exodus 34:29 – 35.)

What impact did Moses' communion with God have on the people?

How personal was the relationship that God pursued with Moses? (See Exodus 33:7 – 11.)

Faith Lesson (3 minutes)

God actually met with and in effect birthed the nation of Israel at Mount Sinai. He demonstrated his presence and chose Israel to be his partner — in effect, a wife and suitable helper in covenantal relationship. There, at the Mountain of God, he declared the mission for Israel — to be his holy nation and kingdom of priests.

As God revealed himself in thunder, lightning, fire, and smoke, he commanded his people to be holy so that they would present him faithfully to the world. He outlined a code of righteous conduct that would extend his kingdom — revealing his desire to reign in every part of Israel's life. He established religious ritual that provided the forgiveness the Jewish people needed. Above the ark of the covenant in the tabernacle, he provided a place where he would reside among his people.

God became known as the "One of Sinai,"[10] which illustrates how formative his presence at the Mountain of God was to Israel's identity. What God accomplished at Mount Sinai when he demonstrated his presence to Moses and Israel remains formative for both the Jewish and Christian experience today. Only the presence of God working in and through us will enable us to be who he desires and commands us to be — and to do his will obediently as it is done in heaven.

Certainly God works to prepare each of us for the role he desires us to have in his redemptive plan, yet our preparation does not make us capable. No degree, no experience, no accomplishments make us capable. Only God's presence gives us the strength, courage, and purity of heart to fulfill our calling when we face opposition from people who resent the presence of the God of the universe. His presence makes our experiences and accomplishments — and, most important, who we are "on the inside" — usable for his purposes.

Elijah, the great prophet of Israel, proposed a dramatic challenge to all of Israel to renounce their worship of the fertility god Baal and to serve God alone. God sent fire from heaven to consume the sacrifice, the altar of stones, the water Elijah had poured over the sacrifice, and even the dirt around the altar. In response, all of Israel declared, "The Lord — he is God!" (1 Kings 18:39). Even then, Israel's commitment to the Lord did not last. Elijah became discouraged, disillusioned, and went into the desert to die. But God sent an angel to sustain him, and Elijah went to the Mountain of God where God had met Israel centuries before. There, Elijah had an intimate encounter with God and left that experience with a renewed mission. (See 1 Kings 19.)

1. No matter who we are, we need that intimate relationship with God as we seek to follow Jesus and obey him in every area of life. It is not something we can begin to do apart from him. How aware are you every day of God's desire to be in close relationship with you — not distantly apart, but actually present, living with you?

    To what extent do you approach your walk with God, your service to him, as something you have to do on your own — alone — as opposed to doing it with God, as his partner in redemption?

2. Moses actively pursued his relationship with God — spending time with him, asking to know and see him, following his instructions exactly to build the tabernacle so the presence of God could dwell with his people. What steps will you take in your life to seek to know God and experience his presence more intimately?

Closing (1 minute)

Read Deuteronomy 4:35 – 40 aloud together: "You were shown these things so that you might know that the LORD is God; besides him there is no other. From heaven he made you hear his voice to discipline you. On earth he showed you his great fire, and you heard his words from out of the fire. Because he loved your ancestors and chose their descendants after them, he brought you out of Egypt by his Presence and his great strength, to drive out before you nations greater and stronger than you and to bring you into their land to give it to you for your inheritance, as it is today.

"Acknowledge and take to heart this day that the LORD is God in heaven above and on the earth below. There is no other. Keep his decrees and commands, which I am giving you today, so that it may go well with you and your children after you and that you may live long in the land the LORD your God gives you for all time."

Then pray, asking God to make us more aware of his unfathomable love for us. Ask that we would be more faithful in love and service *with* him — not just *to* him. Thank him for not giving up on us, just as he didn't give up on the Israelites when they sinned against him. Thank him that, just as he met the Hebrews intimately at Mount Sinai — including Moses and Elijah — he also draws us to himself and meets us. Pray that what you learned today will help you to grow in a deeper relationship that invites people who do not know God to meet him and discover what it means to be restored to the Father. In the name of Jesus, amen.

Memorize

> *They will know that I am the LORD their God, who brought them out of Egypt so that I might dwell among them. I am the LORD their God.*
>
> **Exodus 29:46**

The Kingdom of Heaven Advances: Reclaiming What Belongs to God

In-Depth Personal Study Sessions

Study 1 | God's Presence Among His People

The Very Words of God

> In all the travels of the Israelites, whenever the cloud lifted from above the tabernacle, they would set out; but if the cloud did not lift, they did not set out — until the day it lifted. So the cloud of the LORD was over the tabernacle by day, and fire was in the cloud by night, in the sight of all the Israelites during all their travels.
>
> *Exodus 40:36 – 38*

Bible Discovery

A Place for God to Dwell Among His People

After God's powerful demonstration of his presence with Israel at Mount Sinai, his people responded with awe and joy. They entered into a covenant relationship with him, becoming his partners in his plan of redemption. But God never intended his people to stay at Mount Sinai. Their mission was to move forward and take possession of the Promised Land where they would be God's living witnesses to the world. They would be his kingdom of priests who would make him known so that all people might one day be restored to relationship with God.

So while Mount Sinai marked a pivotal event in the history of the Jewish people — the giving of the Torah — God never told his people to return to that mountain to seek his presence. In fact, God instructed them to seek his presence on another mountain, the "place he will choose as a dwelling for his Name."[11] But how would God be present with his people — his bride — on the way to the Promised Land? Their awareness of what had happened at Mount Sinai would fade with time. They would need more than memories of his awesome presence to face the challenges of their journey.

How would God maintain an intimate relationship with his people? How would he create a community in which his presence lived among them? God gave Moses instructions for building a sanctuary for him, a holy place where he could live among his people. There he would speak to them and receive sacrifices to atone for their sins so they could fulfill their mission of extending his reign by obediently submitting to his will. For the journey ahead, they would construct the tabernacle, a portable tent shrine to take with them.[12] Then, in the same pattern, they would construct a permanent "house" or temple where God's presence would dwell. In the holiest part of his sanctuary or house, the God of heaven would be present with them.

1. After Moses and the elders of Israel went up to commune with God, God again called Moses to climb Mount Sinai to meet with him. In what ways did God demonstrate his presence on the mountain, and for how long was Moses with him? (See Exodus 24:15 – 17.)

    What did God then tell and show Moses that the people were to make for him? (See Exodus 25:8 – 9; 26:30.)

For which purposes did God want his people to build the tabernacle, and what did it reinforce about the kind of relationship God desires to have with his people? (See Exodus 25:8 – 9; 29:42 – 46)?

2. After God's people completed construction of the tabernacle and the priests made offerings to atone for the people's sins, how did God confirm that his presence was among them? (See Exodus 40:34 – 38; Leviticus 9:23 – 24.)

How did the people respond, and in what ways is that like or unlike what you would have expected?

What did God do that showed he was with them — in a day-to-day, life-engaging relationship — all the time?

3. As Israel left the Mountain of God at Sinai, what instructions did God give regarding where and how they were to worship and seek his presence in the future? (See Deuteronomy 12:5 – 7, 13 – 14; 14:23; 16:2, 9 – 17.)

FOR GREATER UNDERSTANDING
The Mountain of God, or Mountain of the Lord

There are two mountains in Israel's experience that are referred to as the Mountain of God (in some instances, Lord). Although no one knows exactly where it is, we are familiar with what happened between God and his people at Mount Sinai (also called Mount Horeb) when God established the covenant relationship with his chosen people whom he had redeemed from slavery in Egypt. At Mount Sinai, God revealed his presence among his people in fire, thunder, voice, and clouds, and then moved his presence into the portable tabernacle built for him by the community of God's people. Then God's people moved on and never returned to that place.

But long before the exodus, God brought Abraham to Mount Moriah.[13] At first, Mount Moriah was the name for a general area three days' walk from Hebron; then it became a specific mountaintop where God's people encountered his presence. The Moriah ridge is in the Judah Mountains between two valleys, the Kidron and the Tyropoean. The ridge is approximately a half mile from north to south and approximately five hundred yards from east to west. It is about two hundred feet lower than the mountains surrounding it.

In terms of the history of God's people, Mount Moriah became the geographical and religious center of life for the Jewish people. It is known as the place where Abraham was to sacrifice his son Isaac to the Lord. But when Abraham showed himself to be obedient, the Lord mercifully provided another sacrifice and affirmed his covenant relationship with Abraham. The threshing floor of Araunah on Mount Moriah is where God commanded

David to build an altar and make a sacrifice for his sin of taking a census of Israel's fighting men.[14] That location was selected by David as the place where Solomon would build the "House of the Lord" — the temple where all of God's people would come to receive cleansing from sin and experience his divine presence. In keeping with its history, Mount Moriah was also where Jesus, the Lamb of God, was sacrificed for the sins of all of humanity. Not long after, it again became the location for a mighty demonstration of God's presence during Pentecost when God's Spirit left the temple and rested on Jesus' disciples.

MOUNT MORIAH RIDGE VIEWED FROM THE MOUNT OF OLIVES EAST OF JERUSALEM. THE RIDGE LIES BELOW THE LARGE FLAT WALLED AREA OF THE TEMPLE MOUNT. THE DOME IN THE CENTER IS A MUSLIM SHRINE THAT HAS BEEN BUILT WHERE SOLOMON BUILT THE HOUSE OF THE LORD THAT STOOD THROUGHOUT BIBLICAL TIMES.

4. No doubt Abraham was stunned when God tested him by asking him to sacrifice his son — the son God had promised in order to fulfill his covenant with Abraham. Believing that the God he served could even raise Isaac from the dead in order to keep that promise,[15] Abraham obeyed. Where did God tell Abraham to go for the sacrifice? (See Genesis 22:1 – 2, 6 – 18.)

How did God reveal his presence and reaffirm his relationship with Abraham during that very personal encounter with the aged patriarch and his young son?

What did Abraham call that place, and what does it reveal about his confidence and trust in his relationship with God?

DID YOU KNOW?

In Christian belief, the ram God provided as a substitute sacrifice for Isaac became a picture of Jesus' sacrificial death. Just as the ram spared Isaac, all who believe in Jesus are redeemed through Jesus' sacrifice on the cross. God met Abraham in the most personal way, demonstrating how a substitute would be provided for those who follow the Lord. That substitute would come from Abraham's descendants, a fulfillment of his God-given mission. This amazing moment pointed to the coming Messiah who would be "sacrificed" at the foot of the same Mountain of God.

---

5. After David sinned by taking a census of Israel's fighting men instead of trusting in God's provision, how did God reveal his presence and forgiveness to David? (See 2 Samuel 24:18 – 25; 1 Chronicles 21:18 – 25.)

The name of the place God selected for David to make his sacrifice was the stone threshing floor of Araunah on Mount Moriah. In light of David's sin, what do you think about what Abraham had called that same place? (See Genesis 22:14.)

What did King David prepare to build on the threshing floor he purchased from Araunah, and who did God choose[16] to build it? (See 1 Chronicles 22:1; 28:2 – 10; 2 Chronicles 3:1.)

FOR GREATER UNDERSTANDING
God's Temple or God's House?

Most English translations use the word *temple* to describe the structure built on the threshing floor of Araunah. This is true of the one Solomon built that scholars call the First Temple as well as the one rebuilt by Ezra and Nehemiah and renovated by Herod (the Second Temple). Although there are examples in the Hebrew Text in which the building is literally called "temple" (Hebrew: *hekhal*; as in 2 Chronicles 26:16), more often the place of God's presence is called "the House" (Hebrew: *bayit*). Throughout history, Jewish people have referred to their temple as "the House of the Lord," implying that God lived in a house among the houses of his people.

New Testament Greek manuscripts commonly designate God's House as "the temple," although there are hints that the Hebrew meaning is not *temple* but *house*. For example, in his address to the Sanhedrin following his arrest, Stephen referred to the temple as "the House of the Lord" (Acts 7:47, 49). And when the disciples heard the sound of a wind that filled "the house" in the Pentecost story, the location is likely the "House of the Lord" and not the upper room as traditionally believed (Acts 2:1 – 2).

6. The tabernacle was the first place where God and his people would meet. The temple, or House of the Lord, was the next step in restoring God's presence to a sinful world. It would provide a more permanent place where the presence of God would become known to all nations — an invitation to seek out God's people in order to experience God's presence. What does Zechariah 8:20 – 23 indicate about the potential power and impact that the message of God dwelling among his people has among those who don't know him?

7. Second Chronicles 5:1 – 14 describes bringing the ark of the covenant into the temple, which Solomon described as a "magnificent" place for God "to dwell forever" (2 Chronicles 6:1 – 2). What did the priests do, and what happened that indicated God was present and in relationship with them? (See 2 Chronicles 5:13 – 14.)

8. All of Israel came to Jerusalem to participate in the dedication of the temple. After Solomon's prayer, what happened that indicated God was present? (See 2 Chronicles 7:1 – 3.)

In what ways was this like what had happened at Mount Sinai and the dedication of the tabernacle, and what did the response of the people indicate about their relationship with God?

What followed Solomon's prayer, and how do you think it affected the relationship of the people of Israel with their God? (See 2 Chronicles 7:4 – 10.)

QUOTE TO PONDER

"And the Temple … was the place where heaven and earth met. It was the place where God lived. Or, more precisely, the place on earth where God's presence intersected with human, this world reality."[17]

Reflection

After the temple was completed, Solomon offered a dedication prayer to the Lord (2 Chronicles 6:12 – 42). Take time to read this prayer and consider the relationship he recognizes between God and his people, particularly as God's presence with his people draws others to seek him. Notice how highly Solomon valued God's presence and his faithfulness to his people. Notice what Solomon asks God for on behalf of his people. Notice his concern for redemption both for the foreigner who does not know God and for God's people who turn away from his ways.

What kind of relationship did Solomon seek to have with God, and, based on God's response, what kind of relationship did God desire (2 Chronicles 7:12 – 22)?

What kind of relationship do you seek with God, and what concerns do you share with him in prayer because of the intimacy of that relationship?

In some sense, God's people today are like the "Mountain of the Lord." We are the place where God's presence dwells so that other Jesus-followers and those who are not in God's family can experience him and receive the forgiveness available through Jesus' sacrifice on the cross.

Considering how important the tabernacle and temple were to the community of God's people and their witness to the world, how important is God's living presence in us, and what impact does it have on people we encounter in life?

What might you or your faith community do to more effectively display God's presence and have a greater impact on people who do not know him?

Memorize

When Solomon finished praying, fire came down from heaven and consumed the burnt offering and the sacrifices, and the glory of the LORD *filled the temple. The priests could not enter the temple of the* LORD *because the glory of the* LORD *filled it. When all the Israelites saw the fire coming down and the glory of the* LORD *above the temple, they knelt on the pavement with their faces to the ground, and they worshiped and gave thanks to the* LORD*, saying,*

> *"He is good; his love endures forever."*
>
> *2 Chronicles 7:1 – 3*

Study 2 | Jesus Tabernacled Among Us

The Very Words of God

The Word became flesh and made his dwelling among us. We have seen his glory, the glory of the one and only Son, who came from the Father, full of grace and truth.

> *John 1:14*

Bible Discovery

If You Had Known Me . . .

Visiting the Temple Mount today — where God's presence intersected with human experience — can be intensely spiritual. If the biblical record had ended after God entered "his House" — the temple on Mount Moriah — that's where people might still have to go to enter God's presence and receive his forgiveness. But God did not limit his presence to that sacred mountain. He would do much more to restore the intimate, personal relationship he once had with his human creation.

If the House of the Lord is viewed as God's beachhead into the world as he carried out his plan to reclaim the world for himself, then the next step he took to restore his presence on earth dramatically advanced that redemptive plan. God became one of us! Jesus Immanuel made his dwelling — "tabernacled" — among us. Those who interacted with him experienced the very presence of God.

1. What astonishing statement did Jesus make concerning himself that reinforced his identity as God in the flesh? (See John 14:7 – 11.)

   What did John realize and testify about Jesus' identity? (See John 1:1, 14.)

   What was the evidence that Jesus was the presence of God in the world and that through him God's kingdom had come? (See Matthew 12:28; Luke 11:20.)

2. People were willing to accept some of what God's kingdom, as embodied in the person of Jesus, brought into the world — the healing of the sick, casting out of demons, miraculous feeding of multitudes, even the raising of the dead. But he did one thing that clearly demonstrated God's reign and stirred up opposition against him. (See Mark 2:1 – 12; Luke 7:36 – 50.)

   a. What implications of Jesus forgiving a person's sins — in terms of the identity he claimed and the ministry of God's presence in the temple — led his audiences to respond so strongly?

b. What impact did Jesus' extension of God's forgiveness have on the woman he forgave, and why?

3. Before the Hebrews left Mount Sinai, the Mountain of the Lord where they received the Torah, God instructed them to seek his presence by participating in three annual pilgrim festivals — Passover, Shavuoth (Pentecost), and Sukkot (Tabernacles).[18] These pilgrimages reminded them of their exodus journey to Sinai, helped to prepare his people for the new "Mountain of the Lord" to which he would lead them, and helped to prepare the setting for the ministry of Jesus.

a. As a Torah-observant Jew, Jesus made these regular pilgrimages — as a child traveling to Jerusalem and back three times a year (more than 110 miles each way) and as a rabbi from Capernaum (more than 125 miles each way). What happened when Jesus was twelve years old and his family went to Jerusalem to celebrate Passover, and what does it reveal about Jesus' understanding of his identity and his intent in fulfilling his mission? (See Luke 2:41 – 52.)

b. The Feast of Tabernacles (Sukkot) celebrated the end of the Israelites' forty years of wandering before being allowed to enter the Promised Land. Coming right after the fall harvest of figs, pomegranates, dates, and grapes, and just before the olive harvest, it was a time of celebration and praise for God's provision of the land he had promised and its bounty. It was the one feast where God's people were commanded to "rejoice,"[19] and they did so with great enthusiasm.

The celebration came at the end of the dry season, so it was coupled with fervent prayer for the coming rainy season to provide next year's harvest. The priests held a water ceremony during which the Israelites would chant, "Hosanna, O LORD, save us," a prayer for God to send rain. At this time, what invitation did Jesus shout in the temple, what was he saying about his identity, and what impact do you think it had on those who heard it at that moment, in that setting? (See Isaiah 12:3; John 7:1 – 18, 37 – 44.)

c. The most momentous events in the life of Jesus among us happened during the festival of Passover. Passover combined three of the feasts instituted in the Torah: Passover, Unleavened Bread, and Firstfruits. Jesus entered Jerusalem with great celebration from the people on the day the lamb was chosen for Passover.[20] He instituted the Lord's Supper during the Seder meal.[21] He shed his blood as the sacrifice for sin on Passover,[22] was buried as Unleavened Bread approached,[23] and was raised on Firstfruits.[24] In what ways does God's perfect planning over time encourage you to be a willing, committed, and hopeful participant in God's efforts to redeem his broken world?

Reflection

Imagine what religious Jews experienced during the time Jesus "tabernacled" on earth. They knew that God demonstrated his presence at Mount Sinai (Horeb) and Mount Moriah — the two "Mountains of God." They knew that God's presence had come to them with fire, cloud, thunder, and voice. And certainly, knowing that God's presence resided in the temple, they had become quite familiar with the sacrifices for forgiveness of sin. Then Jesus showed up and declared, through word and action, that *he* was the Son of God and that wherever he was people could experience God right there, at that moment! Through his presence and redemptive actions, Jesus enabled sinful human beings to be in close relationship with the holy God and live in obedient submission to him.

Consider God's detailed preparation and desire for redeemed "partners" who would undertake the restoration of his lost family members. Jesus could have reached the entire world himself, to say nothing of the legions of angels God has at his disposal. But God wanted ordinary people to be his kingdom of priests, proclaiming the coming of the kingdom and demonstrating him in words and actions to all nations. So Jesus invited them — as God had the ancient Israelites — to partner with him in bearing God's presence to those who do not yet know him.

How can we, who have been redeemed and call ourselves followers of Jesus, do anything less than fully devote ourselves to the redemptive mission God has called us to be a part of?

> Think about what people who interacted with Jesus experienced by being in the very presence of God. How might we approach our mission differently if we viewed Jesus, who walked among human beings on earth in much the same way as God walked with Adam and Eve in the Garden of Eden, as being with us — not as a judge or taskmaster — but simply because he loves us and wants to bring us into his kingdom where we can be in relationship with him?

Sometimes people in the community of believers have a bleak outlook on the future and the difference they can make in extending God's kingdom on earth. But because Jesus is King of kings and Lord of lords, his kingdom will not fail.

What trap mentioned in Jeremiah 2:13 will cause us as individuals to fail in fulfilling our mission?

In keeping with Isaiah's prophecy in Isaiah 32:2 and the dire warning of Jeremiah 2:13, why is it so important for us — God's kingdom of priests in the world — to have drunk deeply of Jesus' living water (John 7:37 – 39) so that we can be a stream of living water on his behalf for broken, hurting people?

What confidence, hope, and optimism can we have in fulfilling our mission because Jesus is enthroned in heaven and is our source of living water?

Memorize

For he has rescued us from the dominion of darkness and brought us into the kingdom of the Son he loves, in whom we have redemption, the forgiveness of sins.

Colossians 1:13 – 14

Study 3 | God's Presence on the Move!

The Very Words of God

When the day of Pentecost came, they were all together in one place.
Suddenly a sound like the blowing of a violent wind came from heaven
and filled the whole house where they were sitting. They saw what
seemed to be tongues of fire that separated and came to rest on each of
them. All of them were filled with the Holy Spirit and began to speak in
other tongues as the Spirit enabled them.

Acts 2:1 – 4

Bible Discovery

God's People Become His Temple

No event has been more significant for the ministry of the church
than what happened on Shavuot (Pentecost) the year Jesus was
crucified, rose from the dead, and ascended to heaven. So much
has been written through the centuries in an attempt to explain
the meaning and significance of being "filled with the Spirit." We
as Christians can learn much from the Jewish setting of Shavuot in
which these events took place.

God carefully planned the coming of his Spirit to occur in a context
people would understand. The followers of Jesus were to be God's
community. Their teacher, applying the Torah in light of Jesus'
work, was to be the Spirit of God. When the Spirit applies God's
teaching to the hearts of people, there will always be life. As Christians, we are in the tradition of Sinai, and Shavuot declares that
God's Spirit brings us life.

Shavuot for the believers was as foundational and formative as the
Sinai events had been for God's congregation, Israel. Israel's mission
was to be a living witness so that all nations would come to that
mountain to seek the God of Israel and live according to his ways. At
Pentecost, described in the book of Acts of the Apostles, God under-
took yet another miraculous action. He moved his presence into
Jesus' followers so that, in a sense, his people became the Mountain
of the Lord that could go out into the world to be his message.

The disciples' final journey with Jesus to Jerusalem must have been amazing. From the fear and confusion they displayed at Jesus' arrest to the exhilarating news of his resurrection, from the clarity of God's plan as Jesus taught them for forty days to his ascension, they must have been reeling from their new understanding of what they thought they had known. They now knew they were to make disciples, to go to the ends of the earth, not simply to bear witness but to live out the kingdom of heaven in such a way as to lead others to imitate them ... to become *their* disciples and hence disciples of Jesus.

But despite all their preparation, they were not quite ready. They needed one more thing. So they went back to Jerusalem as Jesus had told them, to the place where God's presence resided, and they waited.

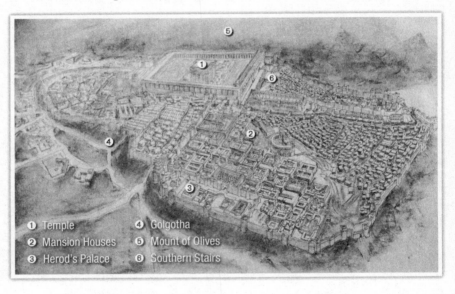

① Temple   ④ Golgotha
② Mansion Houses   ⑤ Mount of Olives
③ Herod's Palace   ⑥ Southern Stairs

1. When Jesus' disciples left the Mount of Olives after his ascension, where did they go — as Jesus commanded and God had chosen? (See Deuteronomy 16:1, 9 – 12; Luke 24:49 – 53; Acts 2:1.)

2. During the wheat harvest festival of Shavuot that followed Passover, at 9:00 a.m. on "the day" of Pentecost when the temple service started, what filled "the whole house"?[25] (See Acts 2:1 – 2.)

What kind of "harvest" did Jesus speak of in relationship to his kingdom? (See Matthew 9:37 – 38; Luke 10:1 – 2; John 4:34 – 38.)

In what way did Jesus' promise that the harvest was "plentiful" (or "ripe") come true on Shavuot when about three thousand people believed and were brought to God — probably in the temple? (See Acts 2:41.)

FOR GREATER UNDERSTANDING
Where Were the Disciples?

Church tradition places Pentecost in an "upper room" somewhere in Jerusalem, but a careful study of the Text indicates that those events took place at the temple. Let's consider what Scripture tells us.

It was the first day of Pentecost week, and Peter says that it was 9:00 a.m. (Acts 2:14 – 15), the time of the Pentecost service in the temple. As it was the first day of the celebration, it was the day everyone came to the temple. Most likely the crowds and the disciples were in the temple courts when Shavuot ceremonies were conducted. It is interesting to note that some scholars believe that during the ceremony, selected passages were read describing God's appearance on Mount Sinai (in thunder, lightning, fire, and smoke) and Ezekiel's vision of God's appearance (with the sound of wind and with fire).

It is unlikely that 120 Jesus followers were meeting in an "upper room" that is not mentioned in the Text. Where besides the temple courts would three thousand people have gathered? And where would that many people have been baptized after hearing the disciples' teachings? There were very few places with enough water for that many baptisms. The *mikvoth,* ritual baths used by worshipers for cleansing before they entered the temple grounds, were near the Southern Stairs, the pilgrim entrance to the Temple Mount.

The appearance of fire parallels the coming of God's presence at Mount Sinai and at the dedications of the tabernacle and temple (House of the Lord), so it makes sense that the event took place in or in close proximity to God's House.

3. What did people see when God's presence moved from the "House of the Lord" — the temple on Temple Mount — to Jesus' disciples, and what other evidence was there that God was doing something very big? (See Acts 2:1 – 4, 29 – 39.)

Where else had God used such a miraculous symbol of his presence more than 1,200 years earlier? (See Exodus 13:21; 19:18; 24:15 – 17; 40:38.)

Where did both events occur? (See Exodus 24:13; Isaiah 2:3; 66:20.)

What other sensory experience did God's people hear at each event? (See Exodus 19:16 – 19; 25:17 – 22; 40:34 – 38; Acts 2:1 – 4.)[26]

Who was present during both events? (See Exodus 19:18, 20; Acts 2:4.)

Whereas on Mount Sinai God wrote his revelation on stone tablets (Exodus 31:18), where did God write his law as he promised he would? (See Jeremiah 31:33; also 2 Corinthians 3:3.)

God gave *Torah* (Hebrew, "teaching") at Mount Sinai, and after Pentecost what did the Spirit become for the new community of Jesus' followers? (See John 14:26.)

POINT TO PONDER

Whereas the temple in Jerusalem demonstrated God's presence to the world, the Christian community must now demonstrate God's presence to our hurting world. We — followers of Jesus — must bring his love, truth, and redemption to our culture, our communities, and our families. If the people around us are to see and know God, and be released from bondage to the Evil One, they must see God through us. We have received the power to be his witnesses, but it is up to us to do it (Acts 1:8).

Reflection

As a result of momentous events during this Shavuot, God's presence again came to dwell among his people. It didn't come through a vision or in a burning bush or on a fire-shrouded mountain. It didn't come in a portable shrine or a limestone temple. God moved into a new temple, a new "House" — the community of faithful followers of Jesus[27] who became God's new dwelling where his presence — his Spirit — dwells. As God's people left Jerusalem and became part of believing communities in extremely pagan places, God was with them. Likewise, he is present wherever his faithful followers are today. The implications of this reality are profound.

The community of God's faithful people is now God's temple. Wherever the gospel goes and people come to know Jesus as Savior and Lord, God's presence lives. Our God-given mission today is the same one God gave ancient Israel — to be a witness to God's character (his "name") and a light to the nations, to show God's love to those in need, to actively do good works so that those who do not know him will meet him and come to faith and worship, too. God's presence gave the early disciples boldness and courage to speak and live the testimony of God's grace. The community was filled with the Spirit so that wherever they were, God's presence was experienced. In his epistle, John writes, "No one has ever seen God; but if we love one another, God lives in us and his love is made complete in us" (1 John 4:12.)

Take time to read Acts 2:42 – 47 and consider what it reveals about God's people[28] living out their God-given mission and being a light to the nations, making his name known, displaying him accurately to the world.

What do you notice about the concern for others expressed by the early community of Jesus-followers?

How well does the Spirit-empowered community of Jesus today represent God's presence? His love? His healing touch?

In what ways are our responses to needy people the litmus test of the presence of the Holy Spirit in our lives?

Starting today, what steps will you take to live as the Spirit-empowered temple of God and commit to being a more faithful witness of who God really is? How will you express the love and compassion God has expressed to you, to obey God in every part of life and thereby extend his kingdom to a world that is helplessly alienated from him?

Memorize

Don't you know that you yourselves are God's temple and that God's Spirit dwells in your midst? If anyone destroys God's temple, God will destroy that person; for God's temple is sacred, and you together are that temple.

1 Corinthians 3:16 – 17

NOTES

Introduction

1. Genesis 1:28; 2:15.

2. Genesis 12:1 – 4.

3. Exodus 8:10; 9:14.

4. John 8:12; 9:5.

5. John 17:6.

6. John 14:7 – 10.

7. See Acts 1:1 – 2. Jesus "began to do and to teach" in his earthly ministry. Certainly Jesus' work continues in and through his followers, his disciples.

8. Sandra L. Richter, *The Epic of Eden* (Downers Grove, Ill.: InterVarsity Press, 2008), chapter 1; Kenneth E. Bailey, *Jacob and the Prodigal* (Downers Grove, Ill.: InterVarsity Press, 2003), chapter 1, sections 1 and 3. These each provide an excellent description of the need to understand and properly use the cultural setting of the Bible.

9. 1 Corinthians 10:6.

10. 1 Corinthians 3:9.

11. Genesis 12:1 – 4.

12. Matthew 1.

13. Jeremiah 29:4 – 7.

14. Jonathon Sacks in a speech entitled "The Western World and the Judeo-Christian Revelation of God" presents a powerful vision of God working through his people who have little power or influence on their own. I find this idea compelling, given how tempting it is to seek to bring God's will by economic or political power alone rather than by faithful living.

Session 1: Capernaum: Jesus Binds the Evil One

1. Genesis 12:1 – 3; Galatians 3:7 – 9.

2. Galatians 4:4.

3. Matthew 3:1 – 3; Luke 7:29.

4. John 7:15.

5. David Bivin, *New Light on the Difficult Words of Jesus* (Holland, Mich.: En-Gedi Resource Center, 2005), chapter 1.

6. Matthew 12:28; Luke 11:20.

7. Matthew 17:18; Mark 1:25 (ESV); Luke 4:41; 9:42.

8. Samuel Tobias Lachs, *A Rabbinic Commentary on the New Testament* (Hoboken, N.J.: Ktav Publishing, 1987), 161.

9. Robert H. Gundry, *Mark: A Commentary on His Apology for the Cross* (Grand Rapids: Wm. B. Eerdmans, 2000), 77.

10. For an in-depth study of Israel's mission as a kingdom of priests (and our mission today), explore That the World May Know, Vol. 13, *Israel's Mission*.

11. See En-Gedi Resource Center at www.egrc.net, Director's Article June 2003 and "Biblical Dress: Tassels." See also James Milgrom, *Commentary on Numbers* (Philadelphia: Jewish Publication Society, 1990), Excursus 38 on Tassels (Tsitsit). See also That the World May Know, Vol. 3, *Life and Ministry of the Messiah*, session 5.

12. Ezra 6:21.

13. John 1:14.

14. For a more complete exploration of this parable, see That the World May Know, Vol. 13, *Israel's Mission*, sessions 3 – 5.

15. For a more complete exploration of Jesus and his disciples in Caesarea Philippi, see That the World May Know, Vol. 5, *The Early Church*, session 1.

16. Matthew 4:13.

17. Todd Bolen, an outstanding Bible history scholar, has published a comparison of Jesus and Jonah on his blog, http://

blog.bibleplaces.com/2012/03/jonah-jesus-and-talpiot-ossuary.
html. His website, Bibleplaces.com, offers the best visual
resources available for contextual study of the Bible.

18. See Matthew 8:5, 14; 16:16 – 17. Jesus lived in Capernaum
    during his teaching ministry. It appears that he stayed at the
    home of Simon and Andrew who, interestingly, had a father
    named Jonah.

19. Joshua 3:10; Acts 13:19.

20. Deuteronomy 20:16 – 18; 1 Kings 14:23 – 24; Isaiah 65:3 – 5,
    66:3; Jeremiah 32:35.

21. See Isaiah 11; Psalm 2, 72.

22. The topic of the kingdom of God (synonymous with the king-
    dom of heaven in the gospel of Matthew) in Jesus' ministry
    is far beyond the scope of this study, but it was central to the
    gospel message as proclaimed by John the Baptist, Jesus, Jesus'
    disciples, and Paul. For an in-depth study of Jesus' teaching
    regarding God's kingdom, I highly recommend Dwight Pryor's
    Unveiling the Kingdom of Heaven (Center for Judaic-Christian
    Studies, 2008).

23. John 10:20.

24. Luke 8:26 – 29.

25. Revelation 16:14.

26. The term *Beelzebub*, which was a sarcastic name for Satan,
    meant "lord of flies." It originated from *Baal-zebul,* which
    meant "exalted Baal" and was a title for the Canaanite fertility
    god, Baal.

27. Deuteronomy 32:17 (ESV); 1 Corinthians 10:20.

28. Exodus 8:19.

29. Exodus 15:1 – 18, especially v. 18.

30. Exodus 19:1 – 6.

31. 1 John 2:6.

32. 1 Corinthians 10:13.

33. Matthew 6:9.

34. I am grateful for the work of Lois Tverberg regarding the meaning and implication of Jesus being the Christ or Messiah. See more of her study at her website, ourrabbijesus.com (http://ourrabbijesus.com/articles/believe-in-christ-its-not-what-you-think/).

Session 2: Decapolis: The Other Side — Jesus and the Man from the Tombs

1. Mark 4:35.

2. Acts 1:8; 13:47.

3. John 3:17.

4. Genesis 6:5.

5. For an in-depth explanation of the abyss, see That the World May Know, Vol. 4, *Death and Resurrection of the Messiah,* session 1.

6. Anson F. Rainey, R. Steven Notley, *The Sacred Bridge: Carta's Atlas of the Biblical World* (Jerusalem: Carta, 2007), 360; Bargil Pixner, *With Jesus Through Galilee According to the Fifth Gospel* (Rosh Pina: Corazin Publishing, 1992), 42; Mendel Nun, *Gergesa as Site of Demoniac,* published article at jerusalemperspective.com.

7. Matthew 4:16.

8. Genesis 1:26 – 27.

9. Numbers 5:1 – 4.

10. Leviticus 11 – 17; Numbers 19.

11. The Targums, the Aramaic translation of the Hebrew Bible from Jesus' time, says "spend their nights chained to corpses."

12. Matthew 6:10.

13. Genesis 3:1 – 7.

14. John 10:10.

15. John Dominic Crossan, Jonathon L. Reed, *In Search of Paul* (San Francisco: Harper, 2004), 143 ff. While Crossan takes a low view of Scripture, which I reject, his research on the culture of the times is excellent.

Session 3: Crucifixion: The Coronation of a King

1. In Mark's gospel, he uses the Greek *euaggelion*: "gospel" or "good news" five times; the Greek *christos* from the Hebrew *mashiach* meaning "anointed" to refer to Jesus seven times; the phrase "Son" or "Son of God" referring to Jesus' sonship twenty-two times.

2. References in Mark's gospel concerning war in Judea and persecution suggest that it was written in the 60s AD. Several early church fathers attest that the book was written to Rome during the persecution of Nero (64 – 67 AD).

3. Robert H. Gundry, *Mark: A Commentary on His Apology for the Cross* (Grand Rapids: Wm. B. Eerdmans, 1993).

4. The following sources provide exceptional background to this study and valuable understanding of the context of Jesus' crucifixion: Robert H. Gundry, *Mark: a Commentary on His Apology for the Cross*; T. E. Schmidt, *Mark 15:16 – 32: The Crucifixion Narrative and the Roman Triumphal Procession* (Cambridge: Cambridge University Press, New Testament Studies, 1995), Vol. 41; and Craig A. Evans, "Mark's Incipit and the Priene Calendar Inscription: From Jewish Gospel to Greco-Roman Gospel," http://www.craigaevanscom/studies.htm.

5. Traditionally, the Antonia Fortress was thought to be the Praetorium where Jesus was taken for trial by Pilate. Modern research casts doubt on this conclusion, suggesting that the pavement outside Herod's Palace — where Pilate, the Roman governor, likely would have stayed — is a more accurate location. So Jesus was likely interrogated by the Jewish priests in one of the mansion houses, then moved to Herod's palace where he was questioned by Herod Antipas and tried by Pilate. Based on the tradition that Jesus' trial took place in the Antonia Fortress and the crucifixion occurred at the site where the Church of the Holy Sepulchre now stands, most pilgrims follow this route for the *Via Dolorosa*, believing they walk in the footsteps of Jesus. However, the route beginning at Herod's Praetorium and ending at the site of the Church of the Holy Sepulchre is more widely accepted by scholars.

6. Adapted from January 8, 2001 print edition of *U.S. News & World Report*, entitled "The Year One."

7. H. S. Versnel, *Triumphus: An Inquiry into the Origin, Development and Meaning of the Roman Triumph* (Brill, 1970). This work is an extended study of the nature and development of the Triumph in Greek and Roman practice. See also Mary Beard, *The Roman Triumph* (Harvard University Press, 2007), an excellent investigation of the history and place of a Triumph in Roman practice.

8. The mention that Simon, who carried Jesus' cross, had two sons, Alexander and Rufus (Mark 15:21), might appear unnecessary. But scholars have suggested that because the Bible mentions Alexander and Rufus as part of the community of faith in Rome, this may be significant support for the tradition that Mark wrote to believers in Rome who must have known these two men, but perhaps not their father, Simon. See Romans 16:13 and 2 Timothy 4:14 (written when Paul was in Rome). Obviously, it is not certain that this is the same "Rufus" and "Alexander" mentioned by Mark, but that is church tradition.

9. In his excellent essay, "Jesus' Triumphal March to the Crucifixion," Thomas Schmidt describes a typical Roman Triumph and compares it to Mark's account of Jesus' death, noting several parallels in Mark's account to a Roman triumph.

10. T. E. Schmidt, *Mark 15:16 – 32: The Crucifixion Narrative and the Roman Triumphal Procession* (Cambridge: Cambridge University Press, New Testament Studies, 1995), Vol. 41, 2, 3, 7. See Mark 1:32; 2:3; 4:8; 5:27 – 8; 9:17 – 20; 12:15 – 16, especially v. 22.

11. Thomas E. Schmidt, "Jesus' Triumphal March to the Crucifixion," *Bible Review*, February 1997, 34. Schmidt quotes Dionysius of Halicarnassus's account of this ancient myth in *Roman Antiquities*.

12. Near the end of Caesar Augustus's life, a Triumph was held for his appointed successor, his son, Tiberius. He was seated next to the emperor with a consul on either side. After Nero's suicide, the Praetorians chose Vespasian, a general who was

in Galilee fighting the Jewish Zealots during the first revolt, to be the next emperor. He arranged a Triumph and is pictured during the process and at the temple between his two sons, Titus and Domitian. The decision by the soldiers to place a rebel on a cross on each side of Jesus is likely an attempt to humiliate Jesus, who was believed to be righteous by many. Even his opponents acknowledged his character. It may also have been an attempt to mock Jews who resented Rome's rule by identifying their "king" with two terrorists who had obviously failed in resisting Rome.

13. See article in the *Journal of the American Medical Association* on the physical process of death by crucifixion: "On the Physical Death of Jesus Christ," William D. Edwards, MD; Wesley J. Gabel, MDiv; Floyd E. Hosmer, MS, *AMI JAMA*, 1986; 255(11):1455 – 1463.

14. Isaiah 53:12.

15. Isaiah 53:4 – 6.

16. Mark 15:26.

17. See John 18:36. Jesus said, "My kingdom is not of this world." Sometimes this statement is understood to mean it is not *in* this world. But throughout his ministry, Jesus emphasized that his kingdom was present wherever he was. So, it is better to understand his statement as, "My kingdom is not *from* this world."

18. Note that there are two different taunts shouted at Jesus. The first recalls the words of Satan when he tempted Jesus: "If you are the Son of God" (compare Matthew 27:39 – 40 and Matthew 4:6). Certainly the Evil One stirred up such scorn in the minds of those who were walking by. The other comes from the Sadducean priests, who taunted him with the words of Psalm 22:8: "Let God deliver him" (Matthew 27:43). Did they hear Jesus' recitation of the first verse of that psalm? In their mockery they unwittingly fulfilled Psalm 22:7 as well.

19. One of the most well-known Triumphs was recorded by Josephus, the Jewish historian, who described in detail the Triumph of the Flavians — Vespasian who defeated the Jews initially before becoming emperor; his son, Titus, who com-

pleted the victory and destroyed Jerusalem and the temple of the Lord (and a decade later would be emperor himself); and his brother, Domitian, who became emperor (81 – 96 AD) and was known for brutally persecuting the Jews. Josephus described the Triumph in detail, including the thousands of prisoners in the procession and the execution of Simon Giora, one of the leaders of the Jewish Revolt. See *Flavius Josephus: The Jewish War*, VII. 3 – 7, trans. William Whiston.

20. Mark 1:1 (NIV 1984).

21. N. T. Wright, *Simply Jesus* (San Francisco: HarperOne, 2011), 173.

Session 4: Ascension: The King Takes His Throne

1. Acts 2:33 – 36.

2. Acts 7:55 – 58.

3. Various That the World May Know sessions complement material found in this session. See Vol. 4, *Death and Resurrection of the Messiah*, sessions 4 – 8; Vol. 11, *The Path to the Cross*, sessions 4 and 5.

4. Ezekiel 11:14 – 24; 43:25; Zechariah 14:1 – 4.

5. Abraham Kuyper, from his 1880 Inaugural Lecture, Free University of Amsterdam. This quote is on the wall across from my door in the hallway of Holland Christian High School, where I teach. It has become the motto of my life: "Take a square inch for the king today and don't give anything away!"

6. Few emperors were "deified" during their lifetimes. Caligula and Nero had adopted this title, but their reigns ended badly. Caesar Augustus was believed to be the son of a god because of the ascension of his father — his predecessor.

7. Deuteronomy 10:14; 1 Chronicles 29:11; Psalm 24:1; 1 Corinthians 10:26.

8. For additional study, see That the World May Know, Vol. 8, *God Heard Their Cry*, session 5, and Vol. 9, *Fire on the Mountain*, session 4.

9. 2 Samuel 23.

10. Read Matthew 27:57 – 28:6; Mark 15:42 – 16:7; Luke 23:52 – 24:4; John 19:38 – 20:12.

11. Matthew 16:16.

12. Isaiah 45:22 – 24; Philippians 2:9 – 11.

13. James Tabor, "Heaven, Ascent To," *Anchor Bible Dictionary*, Vol. 3 (New York: Doubleday, 1992), 91.

14. Deuteronomy 34 (especially vv. 10 – 12).

15. John 1:1 – 4; 8:14; 13:3, 36; 14:1 – 6, 28; 16:1 – 5, 10, 17, 28; Hebrews 2:9 – 10.

16. The Bible uses the marriage metaphor to describe God's relationship with his people, Israel (Jeremiah 23:37), and what occurred at Mount Sinai is described as a wedding. Israel's worship of the calf involved sexual sin as well as "spiritual" adultery when Israel, in effect, took another lover (Exodus 32; Jeremiah 2:1 – 2).

17. 2 Corinthians 12:1 – 6; Ephesians 3:2 – 3.

18. Revelation 1:1 – 3.

19. Exodus 12.

20. Exodus 12.

21. Matthew 21.

22. Mark 14:12 – 23.

23. Exodus 29:38 – 39. The Text does not specify the exact time in the morning the daily offering was to be made. Jewish history records that in the regular liturgy, the sacrifice came mid morning. The Hebrew literally means between the two "settings," which Jewish tradition determined was between high noon (the first setting of the sun) and sunset (the second setting), so in mid afternoon or the ninth hour of daylight. See Nahum Sarna, *Exodus*, JPS Torah Commentary Series (Philadelphia: Jewish Publication Society, 1991).

24. Mark 15:25.

25. Mark 15:34 – 37.

26. Leviticus 23:5 – 6.

27. Luke 24:54 – 56.

28. Leviticus 23:9 – 14.

29. Matthew 28:1; Luke 24:1; 1 Corinthians 15:20 – 23.

30. Exodus 19:1. Israel left Egypt on the fourteenth day of the first month. They arrived at Sinai on the first day of the third month. Israel used a lunar calendar, so each month is twenty-eight days. So they traveled fourteen days of the first month and twenty-eight of the second month, for a total of forty-two days (or around forty).

31. Matthew 4:17; 5:3, 10, 20; 7:21; 19:23. Jesus spent several years teaching his disciples as well as others. He emphasized the importance of living an obedient life as a participant in the kingdom of heaven.

32. Acts 1:1 – 11; John 14:28.

33. 1 Corinthians 15:6.

34. Exodus 19:1 – 3.

35. Acts 1:1 – 11; see Ephesians 1:19 – 20.

36. Luke 24:50 – 53; Leviticus 9:22.

37. See John 7:33; 8:14; 16:28; Acts 1:11; 1 Timothy 3:16. The Text uses active and passive verbs to describe Jesus' ascension. In one sense, he is taken from this world to be with the Father, emphasizing God's validation of Jesus' person and work. Yet the ascent was of his own volition, thus highlighting his nature as Lord and God.

38. See Exodus 24:15; Daniel 7:13.

39. Exodus 32:27 – 28. The giving of the Ten Commandments and the golden calf idolatry did not fall on the exact day of Shavuot. Yet Jewish thought clearly connected them, so that one of the main emphases of the holiday of Shavuot during the first century was the giving of the Torah — a practice true to this day.

40. Acts 2:41.

41. 1 Timothy 3:16; Ephesians 1:18 – 23; Colossians 3:1. Paul mentioned Jesus' ascension and enthronement often as an indication of Jesus' complete authority over all things. That authority implies that the ascension creates a worldview in which his people believe the Lord has taken charge of all things and that as his will is done by his people and those we influence, his authority is expanded and his kingdom comes.

42. Acts 14:1 – 7; 16:16 – 24; 17:1 – 9; 19:23 – 31.

43. Acts 28:16 – 31.

44. 1 John 2:6.

45. 1 Corinthians 11:1. See also 1 Corinthians 4:16; 2 Thessalonians 3:9; Hebrews 6:12; 13:7.

46. Matthew 5:13 – 16.

47. 1 Chronicles 16:8.

48. Isaiah 42:6.

Session 5: Pentecost: God Changed His Address

1. Aspects of previous That the World May Know studies have been interwoven with material in this session. You might refer to: Vol. 4, *Death and Resurrection of the Messiah,* session 9, "Power to the People"; and session 4, "City of the Great King — The Temple"; Vol. 6, *In the Dust of the Rabbi,* session 3, "The Presence of God"; and Vol. 10, *With All Your Heart,* session 2, "Making Space for God."

2. See Genesis 24:40 for an example of this metaphor.

3. Exodus 19:2 – 6.

4. 1 Peter 2:9 – 12.

5. *Beth ab* is Hebrew for the father's house and refers to the extended family community.

6. See Exodus 6:6; 15:13; Deuteronomy 4:1 – 8; 7:8; 9:26; 15:5; 21:8; Psalm 19:4; 78:35; 107:2; 111:9; Isaiah 29:22; 54:5; Luke 1:68; 24:1; 1 Corinthians 1:30; Ephesians 1:7; Hebrews 9:11 – 12; and Titus 2:11 – 14.

7. The Bible uses a variety of metaphors to describe heaven. On one hand, heaven is an eternal and transcendent place separate from earth where God dwells and where redeemed people live eternally with him. They live on the earth, which has been corrupted by sin and death (Revelation 21:27), and then go to heaven (Genesis 22:11, 15; 28:12; Isaiah 63:15). The Bible also portrays heaven as the presence of God with us that raises earthly reality to a higher level of perfection (Hebrews 11:16). The idea of heaven being the presence of God can be seen in the biblical description of "heaven coming down" at the return of Jesus (Revelation 21:2–4, 10). When heaven comes down, God's dwelling place is among his people as it was in the Garden before Adam and Eve's rebellion. In a sense, heaven and earth become one and the same again.

8. N. T. Wright, *Simply Jesus* (San Francisco: HarperOne, 2011), 80.

9. At the Mountain of God, God took Israel as his beloved bride, a suitable helper for his task of the redemption of the world. For further study, see That the World May Know, Vol. 9, *Fire on the Mountain*, session 5.

10. Judges 5:5; Psalm 68:8.

11. Deuteronomy 16:2; 9–12; 13–17.

12. For a more complete study of the tabernacle and its place in the development of God's people, see That the World May Know, Vol. 10, *With All Your Heart*, session 2.

13. Genesis 22:2, 14. See Jon D. Levenson, *Sinai and Zion: An Entry into the Jewish Bible* (New York: Harper Collins, 1985). Levenson's extended treatment of the sacred mountains of Israel's experience, as understood by Jewish thought, is excellent.

14. 1 Chronicles 21:14–28.

15. Hebrews 11:17–19.

16. David did not build the House of the Lord because God told him he was not permitted to do so. He was a man of blood, and God did not want his house to be built with violence. Eventually a man would build it — the Son of God who came to die and not kill (1 Chronicles 28:2–10).

17. Wright, *Simply Jesus*, 80.

18. Deuteronomy 16:2 - 17.

19. Leviticus 23:40.

20. Matthew 21:1 - 11; John 1:29.

21. Mark 14:12 - 25.

22. Mark 15:34 - 37.

23. Luke 23:45 - 56.

24. Matthew 28:1 - 7.

25. The temple is still called "the House" by Jewish people, referring to God's House. Even in Acts, it is called "a house" (Acts 7:47). See the King James Version, which translated the Hebrew as "house" rather than "temple," the structure referred to as "the house" or "the house of the Lord."

26. Note that the Hebrew translated "thunder" (*kolot*) means "voices" (Acts 2:4). Jewish tradition said that the Israelites heard God speak in seventy languages.

27. 1 Corinthians 3:16 - 17; 6:19; Ephesians 2:19 - 22; Philippians 4:9.

28. I am indebted to David H. Stern for this point. His work, *Jewish New Testament Commentary* (Lederer Messianic Publications, 1992), is an excellent study of the Jewish context of the New Testament. His treatment of Acts 2 is exceptional in providing understanding of Shavuot as it was described in the New Testament.

ACKNOWLEDGMENTS

The production of this study series is the work of a community of people. Many contributed their time and talent to make it possible. Recognizing the work of that unseen community is to me an important confirmation that we have learned the lessons God has been teaching his people for more than three thousand years. Here are the people God has used to make this study possible.

The Prince Foundation:

The vision of Elsa and Ed Prince — that this project that began in 1993 would enable thousands of people around the world to walk in the footsteps of the people of God — has never waned. God continues to use Elsa's commitment to share God's story with our broken world.

Focus on the Family:

Mitchell Wright — executive producer, visual media

Erin Berriman — lead coordinating producer

Paul Murphy — manager, video post-production

Blain Andersen — video editor

Christi Lynn — director, product marketing

Allison Montjoy — manager, product marketing

Kay Leavy — senior coordinator, resource marketing

Larry Weeden — director, book and curriculum development and acquisition

Carol Eidson — project coordinator, business services

Zondervan:

John Raymond — vice president and publisher, curriculum

Robin Phillips — project manager, curriculum

Joel Thayer — curriculum marketing

T. J. Rathbun — director, audio/visual production

Tammy Johnson — art director

Denise Froehlich — book interior designer

Greg Clouse — production editor

Kim Tanner — maps and photo editor

That the World May Know:

Chris Hayden — research assistant. This series would not have been completed nor would it have the excellence of content it has without his outstanding research effort.

Lois Tverberg, PhD

Nadav Hillebrand

Alison Elders

Lisa Fredicks

Grooters Productions:

John Grooters — producer/director

Judy Grooters — producer

Mark Chamberlin — director of photography

Mark Chamberlin, John Grooters, Adam Vardy, Tyler Jackson — cinematography

Kent Esmeier — online editor/colorist

Alan Arroyo — assistant editor

Paul Wesselink — re-recording mixer and sound design

Christian Nikkel, Aleece Cook — additional sound

Carlos Martinez — orchestrations

Brittany Grooters, Jordyn Osburn, Hannah Dozeman, Hollie Noble — post-production assistants

Dave Lassanske, Shawn Kamerman, Eric Schrotenboer, Kate Chamberlin — camera assistants

Paul Wesselink, Ryan Wert — production sound

Dennis Lassanske, Alan Arroyo, Brittany Grooters, Taylor Wogomon, Hannah Dozeman, Nola Tolsma — production support

Taylor Wogoman, Dave Lassanske — motion graphics

Breana Melvin, Charlie Shaw, Rob Perry, John Walker, Drew Johnson — illustrators

Eric Schrotenboer — music

Sorenson Communications:

Stephen and Amanda Sorenson — writers

BIBLIOGRAPHY

Bailey, Kenneth E. *The Cross and the Prodigal: The 15th Chapter of Luke, Seen Through the Eyes of Middle Eastern Peasants.* St. Louis: Concordia, 1973.

_____. *Finding the Lost: Cultural Keys to Luke 15.* St Louis: Concordia, 1992.

_____. *Jacob and the Prodigal.* Downers Grove, Ill.: IVP Academic, 2003.

_____. *Jesus Through Middle Eastern Eyes.* Downers Grove, Ill.: IVP Academic, 2008.

_____. *Paul Through Mediterranean Eyes.* Downers Grove, Ill.: IVP Academic, 2008.

_____. *Poet and Peasant and Through Peasant Eyes.* 1976, 1980. Reprint Grand Rapids: Eerdmans, 1983.

Bauckham, Richard, ed. *The Book of Acts in Its Palestinian Setting, Vol 4.* Grand Rapids: Eerdmans, 1995.

Beard, Mary. *The Roman Triumph.* Cambridge, Mass.: Harvard University Press, 2007.

Beitzel, Barry J. *Moody Bible Atlas.* Chicago: Moody Press, 1985.

Berlin, Adele, and Brettler, Marc Zvi. *Jewish Study Bible.* Philadelphia: Jewish Publication Society and New York: Oxford University Press, 2004.

Bivin, David. New Light on the Difficult Words of Jesus: Insights from His Jewish Context. Holland, Mich.: En-Gedi Resource Center, 2005. (www.egrc.net)

Crossan, John Dominic; Reed, Jonathon, L. *In Search of Paul.* San Francisco: Harper, 2004. While Crossan takes a low view of Scripture, which I reject, his research on the culture of the times is excellent.

Danby, Herbert. *The Mishnah.* New York: Oxford University Press, 1977, Sanhedrin 4.5.

Evans, Craig A. "Mark's Incipit and the Priene Calendar Inscription: From Jewish Gospel to Greco-Roman Gospel." *Journal of Greco-Roman Christianity and Judaism* 1 (2000), 67 – 81.

Evans, Craig A. "Mark's Incipit and the Priene Calendar Inscription: From Jewish Gospel to Greco-Roman Gospel." http://www.craigaevans.com/studies.htm.

Fitzmayer, Joseph A. *The Acts of the Apostles.* New York: Doubleday, 1998.

Friedman, Richard Elliot. *Commentary on the Torah.* San Francisco: HarperCollins, 2001.

Gundry, Robert H. *Mark: A Commentary on His Apology for the Cross.* Grand Rapids: Wm. B. Eerdmans, 1993.

Hengel, Martin. *Crucifixion in the Ancient World and the Folly of the Message of the Cross.* Philadelphia: Fortress, 1977.

Hengel, Martin. *Studies in the Gospel of Mark.* Philadelphia: Fortress, 1985.

Hillers, Delbert R. *Covenant: The History of a Biblical Idea.* Baltimore: Johns Hopkins Press, 1969.

Howard-Brook, Wes. *Come Out My People!* Maryknoll, N.Y.: Orbis Books, 2011

Jeffers, James S. *The Greco-Roman World of the New Testament Era.* Downers Grove, Ill.: IVP Academic, 1999.

LeCornu, Hilary. *The Jewish Roots of Acts,* Vols. 1 and 2. Jerusalem: Academon, 2003.

Levenson, Jon D. *Sinai and Zion: An Entry into the Jewish Bible.* San Francisco: HarperOne, 1987.

Notley, Steven R., and Safrai, Ze'ev. *Parables of the Sages.* Jerusalem: Carta, 2011.

Pixner, Bargil. *With Jesus Through Galilee According to the Fifth Gospel.* Rosh Pina: Corazin Publishing, 1992.

Pryor, Dwight A. *Unveiling the Kingdom of Heaven.* Dayton: Center for Judaic Christian Studies, 2008. www.jcstudies.com.

Rainey, Anson F.; Notley, R. Steven. *The Sacred Bridge: Carta's Atlas of the Biblical World.* Jerusalem: Carta, 2007.

Richter, Sandra L. *The Epic of Eden.* Downers Grove, Ill.: IVP Academic, 2008.

Ryken, Leland, Wilhoit, James C., Tremper, Longman III. *Dictionary of Biblical Imagery.* Downers Grove, Ill.: IVP, 1998.

Sarna, Nahum M. *Exploring Exodus: The Origins of Biblical Israel.* New York: Schocken Books, 1996.

Schmidt, T. E. "Mark 15:16–32: The Crucifixion Narrative and the Roman Triumphal Procession." *New Testament Studies,* Volume 41, 1995, 1–18.

Tabor, James. *Anchor Bible Dictionary, Volume 3.* "Heaven, Ascent To." New York: Doubleday, 1992.

Taylor, Lily Ross. *The Divinity of the Emperor.* Middletown, Conn.: Scholars Press, 1931.

Telushkin, Rabbi Joseph. *The Book of Jewish Values.* New York: Bell Tower Publishers, 2000.

Tverberg, Lois. *Walking in the Dust of Rabbi Jesus.* Grand Rapids: Zondervan, 2012.

Tverberg, Lois with Okkema, Bruce. *Listening to the Language of the Bible.* Holland, Mich.: En- Gedi Resource Center, 2004. (www.egrc.net)

Tverberg, Lois and Spangler, Ann. *Sitting at the Feet of Rabbi Jesus.* Grand Rapids: Zondervan, 2009.

Versnel, H. S. *Triumphus: An Inquiry Into the Origin, Development and Meaning of the Roman Triumph.* Leiden, Netherlands: E. J. Brill, 1970.

Whiston, William, trans. *Flavius Josephus: The Jewish War. VII. 3 - 7,* Complete works of Josephus.

Wilson, Marvin R. *Exploring our Hebraic Heritage.* Grand Rapids: Wm. B. Eerdmans, 2014.

Witherington, Ben. *The Acts of the Apostles.* Grand Rapids: Wm. B. Eerdmans, 1998.

Wright, Christopher J. H. *The Mission of God.* Downers Grove, Ill.: IVP Academic, 2006.

Wright, N. T. *Simply Jesus.* New York: Harper Collins, 2011.

Young, Brad H. *The Parables: Jewish Tradition and Christian Interpetation.* Peabody, Mass.: Hendrickson Publishers, 1998.

More Great Resources
from Focus on the Family®

Volume 1: Promised Land
This volume focuses on the Old Testament—particularly on the nation of ancient Israel, God's purpose for His people, and why He placed them in the Promised Land.

Volume 2: Prophets and Kings of Israel
This volume looks into the nation of Israel during Old Testament times to understand how the people struggled with the call of God to be a separate and holy nation.

Volume 3: Life and Ministry of the Messiah
This volume explores the life and teaching ministry of Jesus. Discover new insights about the Son of God.

Volume 4: Death and Resurrection of the Messiah
Witness the passion of the Messiah as He resolutely sets His face toward Jerusalem to suffer and die for His bride. Discover the thrill the disciples felt when they learned of His resurrection and were later filled with the Holy Spirit.

Volume 5: Early Church
Capture the fire of the early church in this fifth set of That the World May Know® film series. See how the first Christians lived out their faith with a passion that literally changed the world.

Volume 6: In the Dust of the Rabbi
"Follow the rabbi, drink in his words, and be covered with the dust of his feet," says the ancient Jewish proverb. Come discover how to follow Jesus as you walk with teacher and historian Ray Vander Laan through the breathtaking terrains of Israel and Turkey and explore what it really means to be a disciple.

Volume 7: Walk as Jesus Walked
Journey to Israel where the 12 disciples walked the walk their rabbi Jesus taught them. Examining the culture and the politics of the first century, Ray Vander Laan opens up the Gospels as never before.

Volume 8: God Heard Their Cry
Just when it seemed that Pharaoh could not be defeated, God provided for His people in ways they never could have imagined. Join historian Ray Vander Laan in ancient Egypt for his study of God's faithfulness to the Israelites—a promise that remains true today.

Volume 9: Fire on the Mountain

When the Israelites left Egypt, they were finally free. Free from persecution, free from oppression, and free to worship their own God. But with that freedom comes a new challenge—learning how to live together the way God intends. In this ninth set of That the World May Know® film series, discover how God teaches the Israelites what it means to be part of a community that loves Him, and the lessons we can begin to live out in our lives today.

Volume 10: With All Your Heart

Do you remember where your blessings come from? In Exodus, God warned Israel to remember Him when they left the dry desert and reached the fertile fields of the promised land. But in this tenth volume of That the World May Know® film series, discover how quickly the Israelites forgot God and began to rely on themselves.

Volume 11: The Path to the Cross

Discover how the Israelites' passionate faith prepares the way for Jesus and His ultimate act of obedience and sacrifice at the cross. Then, be challenged in your own life to live as they did by every word that comes from the mouth of God.

Volume 12: Walking with God in the Desert

Are you going through a difficult period of life? The loss of a loved one? Unemployment? A crisis of faith? During these desert times, it's easy to think God has disappeared. Instead, discover that it's only when we are totally dependent on Him that we find Him closer than ever and can experience God's amazing grace and provision.

Volume 13: Israel's Mission

God gave the assignment to His people thousands of years ago: to bring "lost sheep" back into the love and safety of His kingdom. It's still our task today. In this thirteenth volume of That the World May Know®, you'll glimpse the urgency and rewards of welcoming the strangers and prodigals the Lord longs to embrace. Discover the mission that can give your life—and the lives of those around you—greater meaning than you ever imagined.

FOCUS ON THE FAMILY®

Online: Go to ThatTheWorldMayKnow.com
Phone: Call toll-free: 800-A-FAMILY (232-6459)
In Canada, call toll-free : 800-661-9800